CONVERSING *with* GOD *in the* EASTER SEASON

PRAYING THE SUNDAY MASS READINGS

WITH *LECTIO DIVINA*

CONVERSING *with* GOD *in the* EASTER SEASON

PRAYING THE SUNDAY MASS READINGS
WITH *LECTIO DIVINA*

STEPHEN J. BINZ

the WORD
among us®
Press

Published by The Word Among Us Press
7115 Guilford Road
Frederick, Maryland 20704
www.wau.org

17 16 15 14 13   1 2 3 4 5

ISBN: 978-1-59325-199-4
eISBN: 978-1-59325-447-6

Cover design by Faceout Studios

Made and printed in the United States of America.

Library of Congress Control Number: 2012954748

In memory of
Michael V. Aureli
1950–2011
With confident hope in the resurrection of the dead

President and CEO of Arkansas Hospice,
Dedicated to transforming the experience of dying

Contents

Preface / 8

1. Prayerfully Listening to God's Word during the Easter Season / 11

2. *Lectio Divina* for All God's People / 25

3. *Lectio Divina* for the Easter Season: Year A
   Easter Sunday of the Resurrection of the Lord / 36
   Second Sunday of Easter / 43
   Third Sunday of Easter / 51
   Fourth Sunday of Easter / 59
   Fifth Sunday of Easter / 66
   Sixth Sunday of Easter / 73
   The Ascension of the Lord / 80
   Seventh Sunday of Easter / 87
   Pentecost Sunday / 94

4. *Lectio Divina* for the Easter Season: Year B
   Easter Sunday of the Resurrection of the Lord / 102
   Second Sunday of Easter / 109
   Third Sunday of Easter / 116
   Fourth Sunday of Easter / 123
   Fifth Sunday of Easter / 129
   Sixth Sunday of Easter / 136
   The Ascension of the Lord / 143
   Seventh Sunday of Easter / 150
   Pentecost Sunday / 157

5. *Lectio Divina* for the Easter Season: Year C
    Easter Sunday of the Resurrection of the Lord / 166
    Second Sunday of Easter / 173
    Third Sunday of Easter / 180
    Fourth Sunday of Easter / 188
    Fifth Sunday of Easter / 195
    Sixth Sunday of Easter / 201
    The Ascension of the Lord / 208
    Seventh Sunday of Easter / 215
    Pentecost Sunday / 222

Preface

The practice of *lectio divina* continues to grow, not only in its seedbed within the Catholic and Orthodox traditions, but in Protestant and Evangelical communities as well. Christians everywhere are rediscovering the rich potential of this ancient practice. This contemplative and transforming response to Sacred Scripture is bringing about, as Pope Benedict XVI predicted, a "new springtime" in the Church. The teachings of bishops and spiritual masters have encouraged the practice of lectio divina for all the people of God.

In my first book in this series, *Conversing with God in Scripture: A Contemporary Approach to Lectio Divina*, I pondered this spiritual tradition and explored ways in which this ancient art could be cultivated by people in our day. I reflected on the movements—*lectio, meditatio, oratio, contemplatio,* and *operatio*—and suggested ways that readers might incorporate lectio divina into their lives as disciples. I concluded with a few examples of how selected passages of Scripture could be taken up in lectio divina and lead the reader to interior transformation.

A favorable response to this first book prompted The Word Among Us Press to ask me to continue this approach to lectio divina with the Lectionary readings of the liturgical cycle. What follows is a consideration of the tradition of lectio divina during the Easter season and an exposition of the Sunday readings of the Lectionary based in the five established movements of the practice.

As in the previous book, I have created a work that can be used either privately or in groups. Individuals may use it for their own reflective practice, or churches and communities may wish to incorporate it into their Easter journey and mystagogy. It is ideal for liturgical ministers, catechists, RCIA teams and neophytes, those involved in adult faith formation, and all in the parish who are engaged in spiritual growth.

How to Use This Book

If you choose to use this book for your own personal growth, simply spend some quiet time during each week of the Easter season with the Scripture readings of the upcoming Sunday. As in my previous books, *Conversing with God in Lent* and *Conversing with God in Advent and Christmas*, I have chosen to focus on the first reading and the Gospel, as these readings are designed to relate to and complement one another. The five movements of lectio divina will guide you through the reflective process. Led by the Holy Spirit, you can expect to be changed and renewed by God's living word through this ancient practice. Realize that this book is only a guide—you should feel free to follow as many or as few of the suggestions as you choose. For example, don't think that you must meditate on each of the questions provided. You will be led to reflect on whatever the Holy Spirit brings to your mind and heart after each Scripture passage.

If you choose to follow this book with a small group, you will reap the wisdom and support of others, which can be an enormous help in experiencing the transforming power of Scripture (see the chapter "*Collatio*: Forming Community through Scripture" from *Conversing with God in Scripture*). Groups should meet once a week during this liturgical season to reflect together on the Scriptures for the upcoming Sunday, or they may meet immediately after the Mass to continue the prayerful listening to that Sunday's readings. Members should read the first two chapters of this book in advance and, if they wish, may reflect on the questions of the meditatio at home before coming to the group session. A facilitator guides the group through each step of lectio divina, honoring each movement with the attention it requires. Most of the discussion will center on the questions of the meditatio, but the group should feel free to decide which questions to consider and should not be compelled to discuss them all.

Rejuvenate Your Heart during the Easter Season

During this springtime of new birth and renewed life, make sure that your spirit is attuned to the season by experiencing the personal transformation that Scripture can offer you. Harmonize your life with the rhythms of the liturgy by taking up the practice of lectio divina during the Easter season and experience the spiritual renewal it can offer to you. Set aside time to listen to and reflect on God's word, and pray in response to God's voice spoken in Scripture. As he renews your heart, you will experience the joy of the resurrection.

Stephen J. Binz

Chapter One

Prayerfully Listening to God's Word during the Easter Season

During the season of Easter, we read and reflect on the Scriptures of the Lectionary in the light of the Paschal candle. Whether we are hearing the Scriptures proclaimed in the Sunday liturgy or reflecting on them during the week, it is the fire of the Easter candle that guides us. Recalling the column of cloud by day and the pillar of fire by night that led the Israelites in their exodus from slavery to freedom, the Paschal candle symbolizes the risen Christ in the midst of his people as the light of the world. By his light we are led out of the darkness of ignorance, despair, and sin, and into abundant life, discipleship, and witness.

Following the tradition from the ancient Church, this tall white candle of Easter is lit during the darkness of the Easter Vigil and raised three times, accompanied by the chant, "The light of Christ," and its response, "Thanks be to God." With the Paschal candle burning brightly in the midst of the assembly, the Exultet is chanted, ending with these words:

O Lord, we pray you that this candle, hallowed to the honor of your name, may persevere undimmed to overcome the darkness of this night. Receive it as a pleasing fragrance, and let it mingle with the lights of heaven. May this flame be found still burning by the Morning Star: the one Morning

Star who never sets, Christ your Son, who, coming back from death's domain, has shed his peaceful light on humanity, and lives and reigns forever and ever. Amen.

This candle remains lit at all worship services throughout the Easter season, the joyous fifty days from Easter Sunday, the Resurrection of the Lord, to the Feast of Pentecost. After the Easter season, the Paschal candle is lit at baptisms and funerals, signifying the risen Lord in whom Christians are reborn and in whom they die in the hope of eternal life.

In this Easter light, the Holy Spirit formed the Church and inspired all the writings of the New Testament. The four Gospels, the letters of Paul, and the other Christian Scriptures came forth from the Church enlivened by Christ's resurrection. In this divine light, the apostles and sacred writers were able to understand the deep significance of Jesus' life and communicate the word of salvation that God has brought into the world and desires all people to receive.

By the light of the Easter candle, we can see so much more than we could otherwise apprehend because we are now looking at the world with eyes of faith. So let us keep the flame of faith alive in our hearts during this Easter time as we experience the Sunday Scriptures through the practice of lectio divina. With baptized Christians throughout the world, let us respond to the love that God has shown us in the risen Christ and listen for the gifts God offers us in his word.

Beginning of the New Creation

During the season of Easter, we celebrate the fact that God sits on his throne and says, "Behold, I make all things new" (Revelation 21:5). Because Christ is risen, we are living in the time when heaven and earth are full of God's glory. Through our participation in his death and resurrection, we are able "to share in the divine nature" (2 Peter 1:4). Through the Sacred Scriptures and the holy sacraments, we are empowered to live a new life, not just after death, but even now.

The resurrection has declared a glorious renewal for all creation: "Death is swallowed up in victory." Corruption and death can be mocked as a defeated enemy: "Where, O death, is your victory? / Where, O death, is your sting?" (1 Corinthians 15:54, 55). The time of forgiveness, restoration, and victory over sin and death promised by Israel's prophets and sages for the age to come has now come upon the earth through the resurrection of Jesus Christ.

Because the Lord is risen and reigns triumphant, we can celebrate Easter as the season of new life, and, in fact, we can observe every Sunday as the Lord's Day, the day of Christ's resurrection. The early saints and theologians of the Church marked Sunday as the "eighth day." Creation was completed in six days, and God rested on the Sabbath—but at the resurrection God began something new. On the first day of the week, when God brought forth light from the darkness, God began the new creation. With the new dawn of Easter, God ushered in the beginning of a new world.

In Jesus, the first in the human family to be raised and glorified, the promised new age begins. We see in him what God has promised for our destiny—resurrection from the dead and the fullness of life forever. The risen body of Jesus is the archetype for the new humanity of the future. We will be raised as whole bodily persons— the same persons as in our present life—with every aspect of life that makes us fully alive retained and perfected. Though dead and physically corrupted, we will be recalled to life by a new act of creation by God on the last day.

Christ's resurrection offers us the ability to draw upon his power and grace today. He offers us a power for living that can overcome the most difficult obstacles and a purpose for living that assures us that what we do is not in vain. Since we live our present lives in the interval between Christ's resurrection and the day of Christ's coming when the dead will be raised to life, we live now with a mixture of fulfillment and expectation. He is glorified and alive forever, and we can experience his risen presence in countless ways. Yet we wait with expectant hope for the assurance he has given us, the fullness of life in God's new creation.

Resurrection is God's ultimate affirmation that creation matters, that embodied human beings matter. God loves all of his creation and does not abandon these weak, flawed, and mortal bodies he has given us. The bodily life of every person is supremely important and infinitely worthwhile. In God's eyes it matters what we do with our bodies and with the bodies of others. Christ's resurrection offers us a hope that changes the pattern of our living. How we relate to one another is important; whether we are compassionate, honest, reliable, or generous makes a difference. Since our lives are charged with the risen life of Christ, our existence is given new purpose and meaning. Everything we do has eternal significance, and nothing we do in the name of Christ is ever lost or wasted.

The Resurrection Narratives

All of the Gospels describe the finding of the empty tomb and the first appearances of the risen Jesus as occurring in the early morning hours of the first day of the week. Yet each Gospel writer includes different narratives from the tradition of the early Church that describe the disciples' experiences of Jesus' risen life. Each account offers us diverse insights into the significance of Jesus' resurrection, yet none of them exhaust the full meaning of the resurrection.

Human language fails us when trying to describe the risen life. It is like trying to communicate the experience of a wondrous sunrise to a person born blind or the magnificence of a symphony to one who is congenitally deaf. The Gospels challenge us to expand our imagination as they seek to express in human language something we have never experienced, something that we are incapable of experiencing because of the limitations of our bodily senses.

Because the words of the Gospels are too limited to express the reality of the resurrection, we can best enter the experience through adoration and worship. Sacramental symbols, sacred art, musical praise, and silent homage supplement the power of the inspired word to convey the truths of this awesome mystery. Listening to, reflecting on, and praying over these texts prepare us for hearing their proclamation in the sacred liturgy, and the proclamation of the Gospel in the assembly enhances the ways in which we meditate on these narratives and carry out their meaning in the world.

As we listen to the Gospels on the first three Sundays of Easter, we stand with the disciples in astonished joy as they encounter the risen Christ. On the Second Sunday of Easter, we hear John's narrative in which Jesus appears to his disciples and shows them his hands and his side. Thomas' struggle to believe finally results in his wondrous exclamation of faith in the risen Christ: "My Lord and my God!" (John 20:28). On the Third Sunday of Easter, we listen to the Gospel passages in which the risen Lord eats with his disciples, showing the Church how to recognize his presence in the Eucharist.

On the remaining Sundays of Easter, various parts of John's Gospel are proclaimed. The Fourth Sunday presents the Church with passages of Jesus' teachings describing himself as the Good Shepherd: the one who knows us each by name, who provides for our needs, who saves us from evil, and who guides us into new life. On the Fifth Sunday, we hear parts of Jesus' final discourse to his disciples (John 13–15) in which he explains the results of his death for the eternal life of his followers. The Gospels of the Sixth Sunday, also from Jesus' final discourse, describe how his disciples will live a new life in him. And on the Seventh Sunday, we listen to Jesus' "high priestly prayer" to the Father (John 17), in which Jesus prays for his disciples that they may know eternal life, be consecrated in the truth, share his joy completely, be protected from the evil one, and be united as one in his love in order to be witnesses to the world.

The Acts of the Apostles

During the other liturgical seasons of the year, the first reading of the Liturgy of the Word is from the Old Testament; however, during the Easter season, the first reading is always from the Acts of the Apostles. This tradition is a very ancient one, established in the early Church and mentioned by St. Augustine in the fifth century.

We read the Acts of the Apostles between Easter Sunday and Pentecost because it shows the remarkable transformation in Jesus' followers as they come to terms with the reality of his resurrection.

The early Church—its life, growth, and witness—is portrayed in the Acts of the Apostles, and this is what is presented every Sunday of the three-year cycle. The selections for each year show the Church as it progressively emerges in the light of the resurrection and with the power of the Holy Spirit. As we receive this word in liturgy, we recognize that we are a part of this developing community as it grew from a small group of frightened disciples in an upper room into an assembly of bold witnesses to the message of Jesus Christ in the world.

The Acts of the Apostles is characterized by an intense awareness of the risen Lord's presence in his Church as he continues to guide his people from heaven. In the selections for the Sundays of Easter, we learn how the Church was a community of prayer, worship, and deep joy; how the disciples were united as one heart and mind; and how the Church's numbers steadily increased. We see how the believers celebrated the Eucharist together and shared their belongings, and how the good news was preached—first to Jews in the synagogues and later to Gentiles. The readings focus on two of the apostles, Peter and Paul, recounting the apostolic preaching of Peter and the conversion and missionary travels of Paul.

A prominent feature of Acts is the regular presentation of accounts in which Jesus' disciples give witness in word and deed to the message of Christ. These remind us of the price paid by our ancestors in the faith for proclaiming the gospel. Peter, John, Paul, and others throughout Acts suffered imprisonment, beatings, trials, and numerous other tribulations for the sake of testifying to their faith in Jesus Christ as the crucified and risen Savior. Yet despite their persecution, they would not stop evangelizing because, as Peter said, "We must obey God rather than men" (Acts 5:29). The Church must give testimony in good times and in bad, in suffering and in success. In all cases, the community is to "bear witness" to Jesus (Acts 23:11).

An outline of the Church's mission as presented in Acts is found in the reading from the Ascension: "You will receive power when the Holy Spirit comes upon you, and you will be my witnesses in Jerusalem, throughout Judea and Samaria, and to the ends of the earth" (Acts 1:8). The risen Jesus promises the gift of the Holy Spirit, who will enable the apostles to be emboldened and to embark on worldwide missionary activity.

In the days of Jesus and the early Church, the "ends of the earth" was represented by the city of Rome, the capital of the worldwide empire. Its famous road system enabled relatively quick and safe journeys around the empire. So at the end of Acts, we find that Paul's missionary journeys have led him to Rome. The book ends with Paul under arrest yet still proclaiming the message of the gospel. For Acts to conclude in Rome, then, is not a statement that this is as far as the Christian mission had gone. Rather, it is to say that if "all roads lead to Rome," then all roads also lead out from Rome. For Acts, Rome is a symbol of the worldwide mission that the risen Jesus has given to his Church. The Church, as described in Acts, is first and foremost an evangelizing community, a people empowered by the Holy Spirit to take the message of Jesus Christ to the whole world.

Mystagogy during the Easter Season

"Mystagogy" is a Greek word referring to the process of leading those who have been initiated into a mystery into an understanding of its deep meaning and its significance for their lives. For Christians, the initiation into the mystery of the Lord's death and resurrection traditionally occurs at the Easter Vigil, and mystagogy takes place during the fifty days from Easter to Pentecost. During this special time, the neophytes, or newly initiated, are led into a fuller appreciation of the mystery of salvation they experienced in baptism, confirmation, and the Eucharist.

After the Easter Vigil, the neophytes are not simply sent home to do their best. They continue to gather throughout the Easter season. They share their reflections on their deeper life in Christ through the sacramental life of his Church, and they continue to learn. In this way, they are like the disciples in the resurrection narratives of the Gospels and in the Acts of the Apostles. They are learning from their encounters with the risen Christ and growing in faith and love. The Church's period of mystagogy teaches the rich significance of the Church's Scriptures and sacramental worship, drawing out the inexhaustible meaning of the baptismal covenant and the Eucharistic liturgy.

Mystagogy, however, is not limited to the newly baptized. It is a lifelong process of ongoing conversion and growth in understanding for all Christians. Because in the resurrection God has made all things new, the liturgy and Scripture readings of the Easter season work toward shaping a resurrection mentality in all who live in Christ. Whatever burdens us, whatever we are ashamed of, whatever we lament, whatever has broken our hearts is placed before the open word of God whose light streams forth from the open tomb of Christ. Resurrection touches everything and proclaims hope to all. Easter offers us the chance to look at everything with a new vision. We place our trust in God, who gathers together all that is broken, crumbled, torn asunder, or withered away and breathes the Spirit of new life into us. As we cooperate with God's grace throughout our lives, we deepen our faith so that, as Paul says, "I live, no longer I, but Christ lives in me" (Galatians 2:20).

During these fifty days, the Church's liturgy offers us many opportunities to reflect on our Easter faith and cultivate a resurrection mentality. The penitential act is often replaced by the sprinkling of water as a reminder of baptism. The Gloria is sung and the Alleluia is chanted with pure and joyful praise. It is the ideal time to celebrate the baptism of children, confirmations, and First Communions. Families and parishes deepen their bonds in Christ as they celebrate these sacraments. And it is the perfect time to enter the practice of lectio divina, either individually or with parish groups, using the Sunday Scriptures of the Easter season.

Through the lifelong process of mystagogy, we learn to connect word, worship, and witness. Meditation in the spirit of mystagogy must ask challenging questions: How do I understand the paschal mystery today? How can I allow this mystery of faith to transform every aspect of my life? Through this process, understanding leads to loving, loving to commitment, and commitment to a transformed way of living. In this whole process, the Holy Spirit is the unseen mystagogue, the one who guides each of us and the whole Church into truer understanding, loving commitment, and transformed living.

The Great Fifty Days: Easter to Ascension to Pentecost

Because the joy of the resurrection is so great, Easter is not just one day; it is a liturgical season that lasts fifty days. The Church's liturgical tradition multiplies the day of Easter by seven, making a full week called "Easter Week" or the "Octave of Easter," each day of which ranks as a solemnity. The tradition also multiplies this great week by seven, forming a complete season of seven weeks called "Easter Time." To these forty-nine days is added the fiftieth day, Pentecost.

St. Athanasius, the fourth-century bishop of Alexandria and a Doctor of the Church, regarded the fifty days of the Easter season as "the Great Sunday."[1] So the Sundays that follow Easter Day are called the "Sundays of Easter," rather than the "Sundays after Easter." The Universal Norms for the Church's liturgical year describe Easter time in this way: "The fifty days from the Sunday of the Resurrection to Pentecost Sunday are celebrated in joy and exultation as one feast day, indeed as one 'great Sunday.'"[2]

The Great Fifty Days of Easter are divided into two parts: there are forty days from Easter Day to the Solemnity of the Ascension, and ten more days from Ascension to Pentecost. In many places the Solemnity of the Ascension is transferred from Thursday to the Seventh Sunday of Easter in order to emphasize its importance within the Easter experience.

Luke tells us, both at the end of his Gospel and the beginning of its sequel in the Acts of the Apostles, that after Jesus had appeared to his apostles during forty days, he ascended into heaven.

1. Athanasius, Epist.fest.I: *Patrologia Graeca* 26, 1366.
2. Universal Norms on the Liturgical Year and the General Roman Calendar, 22.

Sometimes we, like the apostles, might be tempted to see the Ascension as a departure, but it is actually the opposite. Ascended into heaven, Jesus is now with all of us here today—wherever we are. The question of the angels to the apostles is also addressed to us: "Why are you standing there looking at the sky?" (Acts 1:11). We can't just look heavenward in wonder, for we have all been given a mission by Christ: "Be my witnesses . . . to the ends of the earth" (1:8).

The whole Easter season challenges us to reflect on our role in the Church's mission, but Ascension and Pentecost in particular focus our attention on the call to be witnesses to Christ. This does not mean that we have to climb on our soapboxes at street corners and shout out the message. But it does mean making our faith both audible and visible, expressed in both words and deeds, as is described throughout the Book of Acts. The Church's call today for a "new evangelization" is basically a call to recapture the spirit of Acts. The Easter season offers a good opportunity to rejuvenate this call.

Many times Jesus promised his disciples that they would not be alone after he physically left them. He would send the Holy Spirit to be with them, bind them in love, and empower them. He made this promise on the day he ascended into heaven, and after days of prayer in Jerusalem, the apostles experienced what Jesus had promised. Like a mighty wind and tongues of flame, the Holy Spirit came upon the community of faith, giving those Jesus had chosen the strength and courage to witness in his name.

The Holy Spirit works outwardly in the Church and inwardly within each one of us. The Spirit makes God's outward revelation given in Scripture inward within us, bringing us to an interior conviction that Jesus is risen and alive. At Pentecost Peter was able to proclaim him as "both Lord and Messiah" (Acts 2:36). God's Spirit does the same for us, enlightening us within and bearing witness to the full revelation of God in Jesus Christ.

From Easter to Pentecost, the flame of the Paschal candle, shining in the darkness, becomes the fire of the Spirit, descending upon the Church. Like the burning bush that burned but was not consumed, the fire of the Spirit is not a destructive fire but one that warms us with God's affection and sets us aflame with fervor. The radical change experienced by the fearful disciples when they received the Holy Spirit demonstrates the transforming effects of this divine flame. The remedy for lukewarm, apathetic Christianity is the fire of the Holy Spirit. The flame of the Spirit enlightens our minds with wisdom and enkindles our hearts with zeal.

Chapter Two

Lectio Divina for All God's People

Lectio divina is the Church's most ancient way of studying Scripture. Rooted in the Jewish tradition, the art of lectio divina has been nurtured through the desert spirituality of the early centuries, the patristic writers of the ancient Church, and the monastic tradition through the ages. In today's worldwide revival of this age-old wisdom, Christians are learning how to experience Scripture in a time-tested and deeper way by listening to and conversing with God through the inspired texts.

The only real purpose of lectio divina is to lead us to a personal encounter and dialogue with God. It is not a highly specialized method of prayer or a methodical system with required steps that must be rigidly followed.[1] The ancient spiritual masters always distrusted methods of prayer that were defined too severely. They knew that God's Spirit moves differently in each person and that God's inner work within the individual should not be impeded with unyielding rules. So there is no need to anxiously assess our spiritual practice as if we had to follow it "correctly" to achieve some particular target. There is no goal other than prayerfully reading Scripture in God's presence with a desire to deepen our heart-to-heart intimacy with him. In lectio divina we let go of our own agenda and gradually open our-

---

1. My previous work, *Conversing with God in Scripture: A Contemporary Approach to Lectio Divina*, explains how *The Monk's Ladder*, by the twelfth-century Carthusian monk Guigo II, unintentionally calcified the practice of lectio divina for subsequent centuries in a way that was far more rigidly and hierarchically defined than in the earlier centuries.

selves to what God wants us to experience through the *sacra pagina*, the inspired text.

The five components of lectio divina, which are outlined here, are best described as "movements," as distinguished from hierarchical steps or rungs on a ladder. This terminology allows for a certain amount of spontaneous freedom within the prayerful practice, as was characteristic of the practice in the Church's early centuries.

Lectio: Reading the Text with a Listening Ear

We begin by setting aside the time and sanctifying the space for our reading. We might want to place a cross or an icon in front of us, light a candle, or offer some gesture to highlight the moment. Placing the Bible or Lectionary text in our hands, we first call on the Holy Spirit to guide our minds and hearts in the presence of God's word.

We read the text slowly and attentively. We try to set aside any preconceived ideas about what the text is going to say. We read reverently and expectantly, knowing that God is going to speak to us in some new way, offering us some new wisdom and understanding through the inspired text.

Though *lectio* is often translated as "reading," the tradition suggests much more than ordinary reading. It is more like listening deeply. In lectio God is teaching us to listen to his voice within the words on the page. It often helps to return to the ancient practice of reading texts of Scripture aloud. In this way we both see the text with our eyes and hear the words with our ears, encouraging a fuller comprehension and experience of the word.

Giving our whole attention to the words, we allow ourselves to enjoy the Scriptures. Savoring the words, images, metaphors, and characters, we grow to appreciate and love the text itself. Paying attention to its literary form, we realize that God's truth is expressed in a variety of ways through many types of literature in the Bible.

Biblical scholarship and commentary can help us understand more of the context of the passage by shedding light on what the authors meant to communicate in the text. The Jewish rabbinical tradition and the writings of Church Fathers in the early centuries show us how artificial it is to make a distinction between the study of a text and prayerful reading. Grappling with the text, searching for fuller understanding, can be a prayerful and faith-filled process. The work of scholars can help us probe all the potential the text can offer us.

Finally, we must always ask how the writer's faith manifests itself in the text and what kind of faith response the writer wishes to elicit from us as readers. Emphasizing the faith dimension of a text helps us transcend the original circumstances in which it was written and allows us to see its lasting influence and universal validity.

Meditatio: Reflecting on the Meaning and Message of the Text

The eyes and ears and even the mind are not the final destination of God's word. We listen to the sacred text so that the words of Scripture might finally inhabit our hearts. When we have created space in our hearts for the word to dwell, the sacred texts can make their home in us, residing in the deepest part of our beings so that they become a part of us.

We can begin to open our hearts to God's word as we establish connections between the text of ancient times and our lives today. Either a word or phrase in the text reminds us of something that has happened in our experience, or something that has happened reminds us of the text. In meditatio we ponder a text until it becomes like a mirror, reflecting some of our own experiences, challenges, thoughts, and questions.

When the patristic writers of the early Church interpreted the Bible, they considered their work satisfactory only when they had found a meaning in the text that was relevant to the situation of Christians in their own day. Because God is the author of Scripture, he can speak to the present through the scriptural record of the past. As the word of God, the Bible has a richness that can be discovered in every age and in every culture. It has a particular message that can be received by every reader who listens to God's word in the context of his or her daily experiences.

A helpful way to meditate on a scriptural passage is to ask questions of the text. Some questions will help us make the connections: What aspects of the biblical world resemble our situation today? What aspects of our present condition does the text seem to address? What is the text's message for us right now? Other questions help us focus on more personal aspects of the text that we might want to reflect on in a deeper way: What emotions and memories does this text evoke in me? Where do I hear Christ speaking to me most personally in these verses? What grace is this text offering me? Often we will notice that rather than us questioning the Scriptures, they are questioning us. The text will challenge us to go beyond our current level of comfort and security: What attitudes or habits must I change in order to truly live these inspired words? Why am I so resistant to reflecting on this text more carefully? After reading a passage of the Bible, we shouldn't be surprised if it begins to read us.

The more we meditate on God's word, the more it seeps into our lives and saturates our thoughts and feelings. St. Ambrose, a fourth-century bishop and Doctor of the Church, described this assimilation: "When we drink from Sacred Scripture, the life-sap of the eternal Word penetrates the veins of our soul and our inner faculties."[2] This is the purpose of meditatio. It allows the dynamic word of God to so penetrate our lives that it truly infuses our minds and hearts, and we begin to embody its truth and its love.

Oratio: Praying in Response to God's Word

Lectio divina is essentially a dialogue with God, a gentle oscillation between listening to God and responding to him in prayer. As lectio moves into meditatio and we listen in a way that becomes increasingly more personal, we recognize that God is speaking to us and offering us a message that is unique to our own lives. Once we realize God's call to us, his personal challenge to us, or the insight he is trying to give us, we must answer in some way. This is the moment for prayer.

Our response to God in oratio is not just any form of prayer. In the context of lectio divina, oratio is rooted directly in prayerful reading and meditation on the scriptural text. In oratio the words, images, and sentiments of the biblical text combine with

---

2. Ambrose, *Commentaries on the Psalms* I, 33: *Patrologia Latina* 14, 984.

the ideas, feelings, memories, and desires arising within us. The words of Scripture, then, enter into our prayer language. The style and vocabulary of our personal prayers are enriched by the inspired words of our long biblical tradition. Our prayers no longer consist of repeated formulas; they resonate with the faith, hope, and love that animated the people of the Bible in their journey with God.

So the biblical words that were at the center of our listening become the heart of our response as well. Our prayer becomes a healthy combination of God's word and the words God moves us to say. The rich deposit God leaves within us after we have meditated on his word nourishes our prayer so that it becomes a heartfelt and Spirit-led response to him. When our prayer does not arise from our listening and is separated from the biblical text, it can become excessively private, egotistical, or eccentric. But when our prayer remains close to the inspired page, we know that we are responding in a way that goes directly to the heart of God.

The tone of our prayer will depend on what we hear God saying to us in our lectio and meditatio. When the text reminds us of the goodness, truth, or beauty of God and his action in our lives, we pray in praise and thanksgiving. When it makes us aware of the wrong we have done or the good we have failed to do, we pray with repentance and seek forgiveness. When the text reminds us of our own needs or the needs of others, we pray in petition. In some cases, our prayer may even be a rebellion, a crying lament, or an angry tirade, as we see in the literature of Job, Jeremiah, and some of the psalms. The key to oratio is that our prayerful response to God flow directly from our listening.

The most essential element of oratio is desire. In fact, St. Augustine said, "The desire to pray is itself prayer."[3] Because we are made for God and only God satisfies our deepest longing, the greatest desire of the human heart is for God. Prayer happens at that moment when our desire for God meets God's desire for us. So when we pray, we are speaking with God who knows us intimately, cares about us deeply, and accepts us unconditionally. When we discover an ability and desire to pray within our hearts, we know that it is a gift of the Holy Spirit. In reality, our desire for God is itself the presence of the Spirit working within us.

Contemplatio: Quietly Resting in God

The movement into contemplatio is a progression from conversation with God to communion with God. After listening to the Scriptures, reflecting on them, and responding to God in the words of our prayer, we then enter into silence. Resting in the divine presence, we simply accept and receive the transforming embrace of God, who has led us to this moment.

Both oratio and contemplatio are prayer that arises from the heart. Oratio is word-filled prayer in response to God's word to us. Contemplatio is prayer with few if any words. It is the response to God that remains after words are no longer necessary or helpful. It is simply enjoying the experience of quietly being in God's presence. We no longer have a need to think or reason, listen or speak.

Of all the movements of lectio divina, contemplatio is the most difficult to describe because it is such a personal moment with God. But it is an essential part of the practice and should never be

---

3. Augustine, *Explanations of the Psalms*, 37, 14: *Patrologia Latina* 36, 404.

passed over. In fact, one could argue that contemplatio is the most essential element of lectio divina, even though it seems the most "useless" from a practical point of view.

Moving into contemplatio is always a matter of our receptivity to God's grace. Our task is to remove as many obstacles to God's Spirit as we can: our inner resistance, our fear of intimacy, our awareness of time, our desire to control the process, and our self-concern. We must remain lovingly attentive to God and experience the desire for interior silence. As we feel God drawing us into deeper awareness of his divine presence, we gradually abandon our intellectual activity and let ourselves be wooed into his embrace. The experience resembles that of lovers holding each other in wordless silence or of a sleeping child resting in the arms of its mother.

Though we might think that the movement of contemplatio is passive and uneventful, God's grace is truly at work in these moments, and the Holy Spirit is changing us from the inside without our awareness. In contemplatio, our heart—the center of our being and the place where we are most truly ourselves—is humbly exposed to God. What happens within us during those moments is something beyond our control. Contemplatio slowly works at transforming our hearts, offering us a taste of the divine life that we are destined to share completely. Though there is often no sign of God at work in the silence, his invisible and unknowable presence is working to transform us at the deepest level.

Operatio: Faithful Witness in Daily Life

Through lectio divina, God's word shapes us and impacts our lives. After reading, reflecting, and praying over the word, we should be changed in some specific and concrete way. The change we experience can be as simple as an adjusted attitude toward our work or a kindness to someone in need, or it can be as demanding as an urgency to change our career or reconcile with someone with whom we've been estranged. Operatio is this lived response to the inspired word.

Through lectio divina, we evangelize ourselves, building bridges between the text and daily life. Every biblical text has a call or challenge to those who listen and respond to its sacred words. Operatio is the fruit that we bear from nurturing the word of God through our listening, reflecting, and praying. We gradually realize that the fruit of lectio divina is the fruit of the Spirit: "love, joy, peace, patience, kindness, generosity, faithfulness, gentleness, self-control" (Galatians 5:22-23). When we begin to notice this fruit in the way we live each day, we will know that the word of God is having its effect within us. In operatio we become witnesses to God's kingdom and living members of Christ's body in the world.

Contemplatio and operatio grow together in the heart of one who prayerfully reads Scripture. The word of God draws us inward to that deep place inside ourselves where we find God; it also impels us outward to those places in need of the light of the divine word. Apart from operatio, contemplatio becomes passive introspection. Apart from contemplatio, operatio becomes superficial pragmatism.

Contemplatio cultivates compassion within us. It enables us to see the deepest meaning and significance of issues, problems, and events. Only when we have attained the understanding and compassion that contemplatio nurtures can our action in the world be a genuine work of God's Spirit. Throughout history many of

Christianity's most ardent activists have also been the most fervent contemplatives. Lectio divina helps us to be contemplative activists and active contemplatives.

Lectio divina is not so much a matter of interpreting a written text as it is of seeking Christ and learning to be his disciple. He is the living Word to whom all the other words of Scripture bear witness. Through listening to, reflecting on, and praying with Scripture, our hearts and minds are formed in the way of Christ. As we deepen our relationship with him and develop a personal bond with Christ, our actions become an imitation of Christ and vehicles of his presence to others.

As our discipleship deepens through lectio divina, we seek to be totally identified with Christ. We desire to live "in Christ," and we experience Christ working within us, with our lives animated by his Spirit. Rather than wanting to imitate Christ, we begin to experience Christ working through us, and our actions become more his work than our own. In contemplatio, Christ prays within us, and in operatio, Christ becomes the doer of our actions. In this mystical bond with Christ, we see the true depth of discipleship that lectio divina can create within us.

Chapter Three

Lectio Divina for the Easter Season: Year A

Easter Sunday of the Resurrection of the Lord

LECTIO

ᴧ

Place a cross or icon in front of you, light a candle, or find another visible symbol to help sanctify the space you have chosen to hear God's word. Call upon the same Holy Spirit who inspired the sacred writers to fill your heart and kindle in you the fire of divine love.

Begin reading when you feel ready to hear God's voice. Try not to bring your own presumptions to the text, but listen as if you were hearing Peter speak.

ACTS 10:34A, 37-43

Peter proceeded to speak and said: "You know what has happened all over Judea, beginning in Galilee after the baptism that John preached, how God anointed Jesus of Nazareth with the Holy Spirit and power. He went about doing good and healing all those oppressed by the devil, for God was with him. We are witnesses of all that he did both in the country of the Jews and in Jerusalem. They put him to death by hanging him on a tree. This man God raised on the third day and granted that he be visible, not to all the people, but to us, the witnesses chosen by God in advance, who ate and drank with him after he rose from the dead. He commissioned us to preach to the people and testify that he is the one appointed by God as judge of the living and the dead. To him all the prophets bear witness, that everyone who believes in him will receive forgiveness of sins through his name."

人

We can imagine the joy and resolve of Peter as he proclaims the good news of Jesus Christ to the family of Cornelius. His audience knows what has been reported about Jesus, but recounting it in the form of a sermon evokes the transforming power of the gospel message to convert the heart. After relating how Jesus' ministry had led to his death on the cross, Peter reaches his climactic declaration: God raised Jesus to life in fulfillment of God's prophetic promises of salvation and sent forth witnesses to testify "that everyone who believes in him will receive forgiveness of sins through his name" (Acts 10:43).

The emphasis in Peter's testimony is on the word "everyone." Cornelius and his household are Gentiles, the first non-Jewish family to receive the saving word and become baptized believers. Peter's sermon is the first addressed to a Gentile audience, the people of the nations, demonstrating how the gospel is to be extended beyond the Jewish people to whom it was originally addressed in order to make salvation in Christ a reality for every believer. The Acts of the Apostles then continues to show how the saving news extends "to the ends of the earth" (1:8), to all the nations of the world, through the witness of the apostles.

Peter's sermon draws us into the drama. We know that we are the people of the nations who have been offered forgiveness and a transformed life. Like all the neophytes baptized at Easter, we have heard the gospel of salvation and are called to receive the good news with an increasingly receptive heart. Peter's message not only declares what has happened in the land, but it also recounts an experience in which he has directly and personally participated. Likewise, the writer of Acts wants all of us, his readers, to participate in the experience of knowing the forgiveness and transformation that can be ours through faith in the resurrected Lord.

After pausing to let the words and images sink in, when you are ready, begin reading the Gospel narrative of the resurrection. Read this familiar account as if for the first time, trusting that God will work deeply in your heart through the words of the Gospel according to Matthew.

MATTHEW 28:1-10*

After the sabbath, as the first day of the week was dawning, Mary Magdalene and the other Mary came to see the tomb. And behold, there was a great earthquake; for an angel of the Lord descended from heaven, approached, rolled back the stone, and sat upon it. His appearance was like lightning and his clothing was white as snow. The guards were shaken with fear of him and became like dead men. Then the angel said to the women in reply, "Do not be afraid! I know that you are seeking Jesus the crucified. He is not here, for he has been raised just as he said. Come and see the place where he lay. Then go quickly and tell his disciples, 'He has been raised from the dead, and he is going before you to Galilee; there

*This is the reading for the Easter Vigil Mass and an alternative reading for Easter Day. The reading for Easter Day is John 20:1-9.

you will see him.' Behold, I have told you." Then they went away quickly from the tomb, fearful yet overjoyed, and ran to announce this to his disciples. And behold, Jesus met them on their way and greeted them. They approached, embraced his feet, and did him homage. Then Jesus said to them, "Do not be afraid. Go tell my brothers to go to Galilee, and there they will see me."

At the beginning of Matthew's Gospel, we find Mary of Nazareth and the announcement that her empty, virginal womb will give birth to Jesus the Savior, conceived through the Holy Spirit. Here, at the end of the Gospel, we find Mary Magdalene and the other Mary at the empty tomb, where they are told that the risen life of Jesus has been conceived and brought forth. The maternal womb, the place of new life, brought forth the earthly life of Jesus; now the cold tomb, the abode of the dead, is emptied of its power as the women experience the new life of the risen One.

The message of the heavenly messengers insists that the women not focus on the tomb but find resurrection faith. He is not among the dead, but he is risen to new life. They are beckoned forward, urged to go forth and announce the good news to the disciples. As the women hurry away on their mission, the risen Jesus meets them on their way. They embrace his feet and worship him, demonstrating that Jesus is a real though transformed person, not just a disembodied spirit or vivid memory. But Jesus does not allow them to linger in homage; instead, he encourages them on their mission as the first witnesses and evangelizers of the resurrection.

A new era has begun for the world with the death and resurrection of Jesus. The earthquake that rumbled at the death of Jesus continues to shake the earth, tying together the death and resurrection into one great saving event. The quake points to the world-shattering implications of the paschal mystery, marking the new and decisive age of salvation. Though its magnitude rocks the very foundations of the earth, its impact is not destructive but life creating and hope inducing. And the seismic repercussions of that great event continue to reverberate down through the course of history. For the resurrection that happened "as the first day of the week was dawning" (Matthew 28:1) marks not only a new day and a new week but a new era and a new creation.

MEDITATIO

The readings are meant to evoke our imagination and recall our own personal passage from death to life in Christ. Continue meditating on the scriptural narratives until they become a mirror in which you can see your own reflection.

- For some people the proclamation of the good news of Jesus is just meaningless words. The words of Scripture must meet a receptive heart through God's grace for those saving words to lead to conversion. How can you make your heart more receptive to the words of Scripture so that they might work more deeply within you?

- Peter's preaching to the Gentile household of Cornelius urges disciples to participate in the outward mission of the Church. How can you be a witness and evangelizer like Peter to those who have not experienced the life-changing good news of Christ?

- The Gospel of Matthew, from beginning to end, promotes a culture of life in response to a culture of death. How does the gospel message encourage your experience of the precious joys of life in the midst of the defeating ways of death?

- When given their mission by the angel, the women went away from the tomb "fearful yet overjoyed" (Matthew 28:8). Is it possible to experience the emotions of both fear and joy simultaneously? When have you felt both great joy and deep fear?

- The women went to the tomb "as the first day of the week was dawning" (Matthew 28:1), and they experienced an earthquake as the angel rolled back the stone from the tomb and sat upon it. How do these movements of the sun and the earth express the significance of the Lord's resurrection?

ORATIO

ᴧ

After allowing these Scriptures to touch your heart and stir you to more personal faith in Jesus, express your response to God in prayer. Let the thoughts, images, words, and feelings of your encounter with Scripture overflow into your prayer.

Begin with this prayer, and continue to pray as your heart directs you:

Saving God, I fear the awesome power manifested at the resurrection of Jesus, but I rejoice in the good news of his triumph. Mold my heart to be receptive to your grace as I hear your saving word. Give me a missionary spirit and a desire to be a witness to the good news of the resurrection.

CONTEMPLATIO

ᴧ

In your imagination place yourself in the house of Cornelius where you have heard Peter proclaim the good news of Jesus. Entrust your heart to God's grace, and ask God to bring you to deeper faith and conversion. Let God do the transformation within you.

OPERATIO

ᴧ

Consider how God is shaking up your life and moving your heart through your experience of lectio divina with these Easter texts. How are your mind and heart being renewed through your prayerful reflection on these narratives? What does God want from you during this Easter season?

Second Sunday of Easter

LECTIO

Close off the business of the day and enter a still moment for your time with the inspired word. Inhale and exhale slowly, becoming aware of your breathing as you recognize each breath as a gift from God. Breathe in, being filled with the presence of God's Spirit. Breathe out, letting go of all that could distract you from this sacred time.

Read aloud, vocalizing the words of the text so that you not only read with your eyes but hear with your ears. Listen to God's word with the ear of your heart.

ACTS 2:42-47

They devoted themselves to the teaching of the apostles and to the communal life, to the breaking of bread and to the prayers. Awe came upon everyone, and many wonders and signs were done through the apostles. All who believed were together and had all things in common; they would sell their property and possessions and divide them among all according to each one's need. Every day they devoted themselves to meeting together in the temple area and to breaking bread in their homes. They ate their meals with exultation and sincerity of heart, praising God and enjoying favor with all the people. And every day the Lord added to their number those who were being saved.

⋏

The Acts of the Apostles indicates that the resurrection of Jesus and the indwelling of the Holy Spirit truly transformed the lives of Jesus' followers. In this short summary, we are offered a description of the early Church in Jerusalem, both its internal life and its engagement with those outside its numbers. Four elements characterize that to which they were continually devoted: the teaching of the apostles, the communal life, the breaking of bread, and the prayers. The fact that each of these four is specified by the definite article "the" indicates that these are not just any teachings, fellowship, meals, and prayers. Rather, these are specific and particular actions of the early Church.

The apostolic teaching includes doctrinal and ethical instructions rooted in the teachings of Jesus himself. As new members joined the community, they were offered these foundational teachings in order to deepen their understanding of the way of Jesus that they had chosen to follow. As the teaching ministry was important for the life of Jesus, the apostles carried on his work through the Spirit.

Their communal life was more than just a warmhearted fellowship among believers. The resurrection had truly transformed the priorities and social arrangements of their former status quo. Their unity in Christ extended to their sharing of material goods and a concern about all the needs of the community. Members of the Church were moved to sell their own possessions and give the proceeds to those in need.

The breaking of bread refers to the communal meals, including the Eucharist on the Lord's Day. The Acts of the Apostles continually makes a connection between the meals of the believers and the presence of Jesus. Modeled on the meals Jesus shared during his life, culminating in the Last Supper, the believers continued to gather in homes to worship God, knowing that the risen Jesus was with them in the breaking of the bread.

The prayers were most likely fixed prayer in the morning and evening, in addition to spontaneous prayer for the needs of the Church. They continued to attend the services of the Temple, praying the psalms and prayers of their tradition. In addition, they developed liturgical prayers for their worship at table as well as hymns of praise and thanksgiving.

In essence, the believers formed a learning Church, a loving Church, a worshiping Church, and an evangelizing Church. The quality of their life together earned them the good favor of those outside the community. The Church's witness was infectious, and its numbers steadily grew as God converted hearts and led many to salvation.

JOHN 20:19-31

On the evening of that first day of the week, when the doors were locked, where the disciples were, for fear of the Jews, Jesus came and stood in their midst and said to them, "Peace be with you." When he had said this, he showed them his hands and his side. The disciples rejoiced when they saw the Lord. Jesus said to them again, "Peace be with you. As the Father has sent me, so I send you." And when he had said this, he breathed on them and said to them, "Receive the Holy Spirit. Whose sins you forgive are forgiven them, and whose sins you retain are retained."

Thomas, called Didymus, one of the Twelve, was not with them when Jesus came. So the other disciples said to him, "We have seen the Lord." But he said to them, "Unless I see the mark of the nails in his hands and put my finger into the nailmarks and put my hand into his side, I will not believe."

Now a week later his disciples were again inside and Thomas was with them. Jesus came, although the doors were locked, and stood in their midst and said, "Peace be with you." Then he said to Thomas, "Put your finger here and see my hands, and bring your hand and put it into my side, and do not be unbelieving, but believe." Thomas answered and said to him, "My Lord and my God!" Jesus said to him, "Have you come to believe because you have seen me? Blessed are those who have not seen and have believed."

Now Jesus did many other signs in the presence of his disciples that are not written in this book. But these are written that you may come to believe that Jesus is the Christ, the Son of God, and that through this belief you may have life in his name.

On the evening of the day of resurrection, the disciples have locked themselves behind closed doors, terrified for their own lives and disillusioned after witnessing the death of Jesus. But locks are no obstacle for the One who has broken the bonds of death. The Lord's greeting, "Peace be with you" (John 20:19), moves the disciples from their fearful state to the experience of joy and wonderment. Peace (in Hebrew, *shalom*) is an experience of deep confidence that dispels fear and is full of hope. Hearing these words and seeing the glorified wounds of Jesus, the disciples remember the words of Jesus spoken in the upper room before his death: "Peace I leave with you; my peace I give to you. Not as the world gives do I give it to you. Do not let your hearts be troubled or afraid" (John 14:27).

After Jesus' second greeting of peace, Jesus commissions his disciples: "As the Father has sent me, so I send you" (John 20:21). Because God so loved the world, he sent his Son to reveal the Father for all to see—through his teachings, his healing signs, and his total self-gift on the cross. Now Jesus sends us, his disciples, on that same mission. We are to be for the world what Jesus has been for the world. We are to embody the Father's love, to teach and heal, to comfort and bring peace. And to empower his Church, Jesus breathes on them and says, "Receive the Holy Spirit" (20:22). As the Father had sent out Jesus in the power of the Holy Spirit, so now Jesus sends his disciples in the power of that divine Spirit.

When Jesus appears to them again on the following Sunday and invites Thomas to touch his wounds, Thomas' doubts disappear. His skepticism is transformed into the supreme profession of Easter faith: "My Lord and my God!" (John 20:28). For many, like Thomas, doubt is the pathway to belief. For those who struggle with faith, Thomas is a model. The most confounded cynic can become the most jubilant believer of all.

MEDITATIO

Spend some time reflecting on the impact of the resurrection on the life of the early believers. Let these accounts interact with your own seeking, questions, ideas, and concerns until you are aware of the personal messages the texts offer to you.

- The communal life of the early Church was a visible testimony and witness to their faith for those around them. In what ways is your Church and Christian community a witness to the presence of Christ among you?

- The portrait of the early Church in Acts describes a community in which its members are most concerned about what they can contribute rather than what they can receive. In what ways does the individualism of our culture today undercut the development of this kind of communal life?

- Churches today are sometimes accused of acting as isolated clubs promoting socialization and friendly activities. How can a parish become a truly learning, loving, worshiping, and evangelizing church?

- When Jesus appeared to his disciples, he spoke a word of peace and he showed them his hands and his side. Why did he use both word and sign to bring them to the experience of Easter faith? How do you experience Christ's presence in similar ways?

- In what ways can Thomas give hope to those who doubt? In what ways can he be a model for you in your struggles with faith?

ORATIO

After listening and reflecting on the Easter faith of the newborn Church, respond to the risen Lord as a prayerful disciple. Let this prayer be an incentive to continue with your own:

Wounded and risen Lord, let me know the peace and joy of your resurrection in every part of my life. Empower me with your Holy Spirit, and send me to offer your compassion, forgiveness, and healing to others.

Continue to pray in whatever words your heart directs.

CONTEMPLATIO

As you pray, focus on your breath, welcoming the divine breath of life that dissolves fear.

Imaginatively place yourself in that upper room with the disciples as the risen Lord makes his presence known to them. Feel his risen life dispelling your fears and renewing your life. Make the words of Thomas, "My Lord and my God," your own, slowly repeating them as you rest in the Lord's presence.

OPERATIO

The light of God's word can dispel the darkness of fear, doubt, and disillusionment. As you prayerfully reflect on Scripture, lectio divina gradually transforms you into a disciple sent by Jesus to embody the Father's love, to teach and heal, to comfort and bring peace. In what direction is the risen Lord sending you this week?

Third Sunday of Easter

LECTIO

Separate this time and space from the rest of your day so that you may be ready to truly hear the words of the inspired texts. Read the sermon of Peter aloud so that you will see it with your eyes, hear it with your ears, and speak it with your lips.

Highlight, underline, circle, and mark up the text as a way to focus on your reading. This will help you to pay attention in a new way as you read.

ACTS 2:14, 22-33

Then Peter stood up with the Eleven, raised his voice, and proclaimed: "You who are Jews, indeed all of you staying in Jerusalem. Let this be known to you, and listen to my words. You who are Israelites, hear these words. Jesus the Nazorean was a man commended to you by God with mighty deeds, wonders, and signs, which God worked through him in your midst, as you yourselves know. This man, delivered up by the set plan and foreknowledge of God, you killed, using lawless men to crucify him. But God raised him up, releasing him from the throes of death, because it was impossible for him to be held by it. For David says of him:

> *I saw the Lord ever before me,*
> *with him at my right hand I shall not be disturbed.*

*Therefore my heart has been glad and my tongue has
   exulted;
my flesh, too, will dwell in hope,
because you will not abandon my soul
   to the netherworld,
nor will you suffer your holy one to see corruption.
You have made known to me the paths of life;
   you will fill me with joy in your presence.*

"My brothers, one can confidently say to you about the patriarch David that he died and was buried, and his tomb is in our midst to this day. But since he was a prophet and knew that God had sworn an oath to him that he would set one of his descendants upon his throne, he foresaw and spoke of the resurrection of the Christ, that neither was he abandoned to the netherworld nor did his flesh see corruption. God raised this Jesus; of this we are all witnesses. Exalted at the right hand of God, he received the promise of the Holy Spirit from the Father and poured him forth, as you see and hear."

へ

The speeches of the apostles, which are found throughout the Book of Acts, are replete with quotations from and allusions to the Old Testament, the Scriptures of Israel. These speeches proclaim that Jesus is the climax of God's saving plan and that his life, death, and resurrection fulfill the ancient Scriptures. For this reason, selections from the Acts of the Apostles replace the usual Old Testament reading during the season of Easter. The speeches indicate the early Christian interpretation of the Old Testament in light of the resurrection of Jesus. His paschal mystery is the key that opens up all the mysteries hidden in Israel's Scriptures.

This first speech of Acts, given by Peter, is an example of this apostolic preaching. Peter stands up with the other apostles and calls on the crowd to listen. He presents Jesus the Nazorean and proclaims what God has done through him. Even though Jesus was put to death by the people of Jerusalem, his death was not an arbitrary tragedy; rather, he was "delivered up by the set plan and foreknowledge of God" (Acts 2:23). And God raised him from death, as his saving will directed, "because it was impossible for him to be held by it" (2:24). In this way, Peter expresses the necessity of the death and resurrection of Jesus in God's saving plan.

As evidence of this way of interpreting Scripture in light of the resurrection, Peter quotes a few verses from Psalm 16. In this psalm of comfort, David the psalmist speaks as a prophet because he "foresaw and spoke of the resurrection of the Christ" (Acts 2:31). The One whom God would not abandon to death is not David, who was buried in Jerusalem, but David's descendant, Jesus, the Messiah of Israel. He now reigns with God and pours forth his Spirit upon his Church.

Allow a few moments of quiet to let the inspired words of Peter resonate within your heart. When you are ready, listen carefully to the words of Luke's Gospel.

LUKE 24:13-35

That very day, the first day of the week, two of Jesus' disciples were going to a village seven miles from Jerusalem called Emmaus, and they were conversing about all the things that had occurred. And it happened that while they were conversing and debating, Jesus himself drew near and walked with them, but their eyes were prevented from recognizing him. He asked them, "What are you discussing as you walk along?" They stopped, looking downcast. One of them, named Cleopas, said to him in reply, "Are you the only visitor to Jerusalem who does not know of the things that have taken place there in these days?" And he replied to them, "What sort of things?" They said to him, "The things that happened to Jesus the Nazarene, who was a prophet mighty in deed and word before God and all the people, how our chief priests and rulers both handed him over to a sentence of death and crucified him. But we were hoping that he would be the one to redeem Israel; and besides all this, it is now the third day since this took place. Some women from our group, however, have astounded us: they were at the tomb early in the morning and did not find his body; they came back and reported that they had indeed seen a vision of angels who announced that he was alive. Then some of those with us went to the tomb and found things just as the women had described, but him they did not see." And he said to them, "Oh, how foolish you are! How slow of heart to believe all that the prophets spoke! Was it not necessary that the Christ should suffer these things and enter into his glory?" Then beginning with Moses and all the prophets, he interpreted to them what referred to him in all the Scriptures. As they approached the village to which they were going, he gave the impression that he was going on farther. But they urged him, "Stay with us, for it is nearly evening and the day is almost over." So he went in to stay with them. And it happened that, while he was with them at table, he took bread, said the blessing, broke it, and gave it to them. With that their eyes were opened and they recognized him, but he vanished from their sight. Then they said to each other, "Were not our hearts burning within us while he spoke to us on the way and opened the Scriptures to us?" So they set out at once and returned to Jerusalem where they found gathered together the eleven and those with them who were saying, "The Lord has truly been raised and has appeared to Simon!" Then the two recounted what had taken place on the way and how he was made known to them in the breaking of bread.

In Acts, the crowds receive instructions from Peter about how to interpret the Old Testament in light of the glorified Christ, but in the Gospel, the two disciples receive similar instructions from the risen Lord himself. In both the Jerusalem account of Peter and the Emmaus story, the resurrection is the new light that shines on ancient texts and gives them new meaning.

As the risen Jesus walked along and entered into conversation with the two disciples, he began to interpret the Scriptures, "beginning with Moses and all the prophets." Yet he did not explain the texts like a Jewish rabbi; rather, "he interpreted to them what referred to him in all the Scriptures" (Luke 24:27). Unlike Peter, Jesus did not seem to focus on any particular passage. Rather, he laid out for them the way in which "all the Scriptures" prepare for the gospel and are fulfilled in the cross and resurrection of Christ.

The account not only describes one Sunday evening in Emmaus; it also indicates how the risen Christ continually reveals himself through the Scriptures of Israel with the guidance of the Holy Spirit. The Jewish disciples continually read their Scriptures in the light of the resurrection in order to understand how the entire saving plan of God culminated in the death and resurrection of the Messiah.

Through the Emmaus account, the disciples and Luke's readers realize how the risen Lord will be present to his Church. The encounter demonstrates the dynamic relationship between word and sacrament in the life of the Church, and it reflects the twofold structure of Christian assembly. Both the interpretation of the Scriptures and the breaking of the bread are actions of the risen Christ in which his presence is made real for the Church.

MEDITATIO

Having listened to the writings of Luke in both the Acts of the Apostles and his Gospel, spend some moments reflecting on these narratives in light of your own Easter journey.

- Peter's speech in Jerusalem exemplifies the tone and method of the apostolic preaching throughout Acts. Why do the apostles include so many texts from the Old Testament? How is your understanding amplified when you read the psalms through, with, and in Jesus Christ?

- Reread the verses of Psalm 16 quoted by Peter in his speech. In what ways does this song of David give you comfort and hope? How does it offer you even greater hope when you read it like Peter, in the light of Christ's resurrection?

- Luke places all his resurrection narratives on the same day, "the first day of the week" (24:13). Why is this day significant for the Church's understanding of how Jesus is present to them in word and sacrament?

- Jesus interpreted the Scriptures, "beginning with Moses and all the prophets," and showed his disciples "what referred to him in all the Scriptures" (Luke 24:27). In what ways does coming to know and understand the Torah and prophets of Israel open your eyes to know and recognize Jesus?

- The fact that Luke leaves one of the two disciples unnamed in his narrative invites each reader to step into the shoes of this anonymous traveler. What does the Emmaus account teach you about the ways that Jesus reveals himself to you today?

ORATIO

After listening and reflecting on God's word to us, we respond to God in words of prayer. Let these words be your prayer starter:

Risen Lord, open the Scriptures to me so that you may also open my eyes, mind, and heart to you. Assure me of your presence with me when I study the Bible so that my heart will catch fire and burn with understanding and love.

Continue to pray whatever words well up from the depths of your heart.

CONTEMPLATIO

Imagine that you are the anonymous disciple at Emmaus and you have just recognized Jesus at table. Just contemplate that moment, and remain there for as long as you wish.

OPERATIO

The Gospel begins with the disciples walking slowly and hopelessly from Jerusalem to Emmaus, and it ends with their movement hurriedly and expectantly from Emmaus to Jerusalem with the good news of the risen Lord. For one of the options for the Rite of Dismissal at Mass, the priest says, "Go and announce the Gospel of the Lord." How can I better respond to this final exhortation of the Mass?

Fourth Sunday of Easter

LECTIO

Each of these readings speaks about the way to life. Jesus says, "I came so that they might have life and have it more abundantly" (John 10:10). This abundant life is what we can experience through faith in him.

Begin reading when you are prepared to encounter God through the words of these inspired Scriptures and to receive the abundant life that Jesus desires for you.

ACTS 2:14A, 36-41

Then Peter stood up with the Eleven, raised his voice, and proclaimed: "Let the whole house of Israel know for certain that God has made both Lord and Christ, this Jesus whom you crucified."

Now when they heard this, they were cut to the heart, and they asked Peter and the other apostles, "What are we to do, my brothers?" Peter said to them, "Repent and be baptized, every one of you, in the name of Jesus Christ for the forgiveness of your sins; and you will receive the gift of the Holy Spirit. For the promise is made to you and to your children and to all those far off, whomever the Lord our God will call." He testified with many other arguments, and was exhorting them, "Save yourselves from this corrupt generation." Those who accepted his message were baptized, and about three thousand persons were added that day.

∧

The way to receive the abundant life God desires for us is indicated by this conclusion of Peter's first sermon in Acts. The people to whom Peter speaks are "cut to the heart" when he accuses them of crucifying the One whom "God has made both Lord and Christ" (Acts 2:36, 37). Peter's preaching provokes many to ask, "What are we to do?" (2:37). Peter responds with a clear call for a decision involving a no and a yes: "Repent," saying no to your past life of rejecting God and living for yourselves, "and be baptized" (2:38), saying yes to God by faith in Jesus Christ. Through repentance and baptism, all who enter this new community receive forgiveness of sins and the gift of the Holy Spirit.

From his own bitter experience of denying Jesus and then experiencing forgiveness, Peter knows only too well what is needed to receive abundant life. Repentance is not just being sorry; it is an act of radical conversion of the mind and heart, a conscious turning toward God in order to receive the life he offers through Jesus. While repentance is primarily a personal and interior experience, baptism is a public and communal expression of this new life. Baptism "in the name of Jesus Christ" (Acts 2:38) expresses one's faith in him and the reception of the gift of new life from God. God calls those in Jerusalem and their children as well as "those far off" (2:39) to receive the gift of life he has promised.

Many respond to Peter's exhortation with enthusiastic acceptance, and thousands are added to the community of faith. These form a powerful communal witness to others in the city so that more and more people come to know Jesus as Messiah and Lord.

JOHN 10:1-10

Jesus said: "Amen, amen, I say to you, whoever does not enter a sheepfold through the gate but climbs over elsewhere is a thief and a robber. But whoever enters through the gate is the shepherd of the sheep. The gatekeeper opens it for him, and the sheep hear his voice, as the shepherd calls his own sheep by name and leads them out. When he has driven out all his own, he walks ahead of them, and the sheep follow him, because they recognize his voice. But they will not follow a stranger; they will run away from him, because they do not recognize the voice of strangers." Although Jesus used this figure of speech, the Pharisees did not realize what he was trying to tell them.

So Jesus said again, "Amen, amen, I say to you, I am the gate for the sheep. All who came before me are thieves and robbers, but the sheep did not listen to them. I am the gate. Whoever enters through me will be saved, and will come in and go out and find pasture. A thief comes only to steal and slaughter and destroy; I came so that they might have life and have it more abundantly."

The Gospel features two short parables about shepherds and sheep gates in which Jesus draws on the imagery of shepherding in the ancient world. The first contrasts the good shepherd with a thief or a stranger. We are to imagine a large corral where the sheep are kept safe from wild animals when they are not in the fields at pasture. Unlike a thief or stranger, the good shepherd enters through the gate, calls his sheep by name, and leads them out. They follow him because they know and trust the shepherd. Each sheep responds to the familiar voice of the shepherd, who calls each sheep by its own familiar name. The shepherd walks ahead of the sheep to bring them to pasture, the sheep following the one whose voice is familiar to them. In the case of a stranger, whose voice the sheep do not know, the sheep will not follow but will flee in panic.

In the second parable, the focus is on the gate for the sheep. Here Jesus identifies himself as the gateway for his flock, as opposed to corrupt religious leaders who are thieves and robbers. Jesus is the way through which the sheep are protected and the way of access to good pasture. He is the mediator who will provide for them what they need and desire: both secure protection and abundant nourishment. He came for the sake of his followers, "that they might have life and have it more abundantly" (John 10:10). This full and abundant life is salvation, the eternal life that begins already in the here and now.

As followers of Jesus, we recognize that the gate swings in two directions. We come into the sheepfold through him, and we are led out through him. As we are led in through Jesus, we find a place of refreshment and rest in the embrace of the believing community, a space where our wounds can be healed and where we can be nourished by the word and at the table. But we are also led out through Jesus to find pasture, the verdant space of mission. Jesus is the gate that opens in and out. In both directions is found rich and abundant life.

MEDITATIO

Reflect on the words of these Scriptures in light of your own desire for full and abundant life. Consider what you are being asked to do in response to the words of Peter and Jesus.

- In what way is a decision about Jesus both a no and a yes? Why did so many respond enthusiastically to the message preached by Peter?

- Based on the model of Peter's sermon and Jesus' parables, how would you explain the meaning of becoming a Christian to an inquirer? What is required? What is promised?

- Growing in the abundant life that God has given us in baptism is the spirit of the Easter season. What can you do during these days of Easter to allow the life you received at baptism to grow and mature within you?

- God is frequently spoken of in the Old Testament as Israel's shepherd: "The lost I will search out, the strays I will bring back, the injured I will bind up, and the sick I will heal" (Ezekiel 34:16). Where do you see these actions in the work of Jesus?

- Jesus compares his care of the sheep with the deception of thieves and strangers. Who are the robbers and outsiders who threaten you with harm? How do you experience the protection of Jesus?

ORATIO

It is God's grace at work within you that gives you a desire to pray. Touch that deep desire within you and respond to God in prayer. Speak familiarly to the good shepherd who knows his sheep:

Lord Jesus, you offer me security and protect me from danger. You are the way to the green pastures of abundant life. I repent from following the deceptive call of those who offer me another way to live. I place my trust in you to receive forgiveness of my sins and your gift of the Holy Spirit.

Continue to expose your heart as you pray in whatever way you choose.

CONTEMPLATIO

When the words of prayer are no longer necessary or helpful, just rest in quiet in the presence of the Shepherd who loves you. Listen as he calls you by name, and open your heart to the intimacy to which the Shepherd is leading you.

OPERATIO

Jesus is the gate that swings in two directions: both in and out. Throughout this week consider when you are being led into the sheepfold and when you are being called out to mission. How responsive are you to being led in both directions?

Fifth Sunday of Easter

LECTIO

人

As you prepare for your attentive listening to God's word, call on the Holy Spirit to enlighten your mind and heart as you read the sacred texts. Breathe in, being filled with the presence of God's Spirit. Breathe out, letting go of all that could distract you from this sacred time.

Read these texts aloud, seeking to hear God's word within them, opening yourself to whatever new insight or encouragement God wishes to offer you.

ACTS 6:1-7

As the number of disciples continued to grow, the Hellenists complained against the Hebrews because their widows were being neglected in the daily distribution. So the Twelve called together the community of the disciples and said, "It is not right for us to neglect the word of God to serve at table. Brothers, select from among you seven reputable men, filled with the Spirit and wisdom, whom we shall appoint to this task, whereas we shall devote ourselves to prayer and to the ministry of the word." The proposal was acceptable to the whole community, so they chose Stephen, a man filled with faith and the Holy Spirit, also Philip, Prochorus, Nicanor, Timon, Parmenas, and Nicholas of Antioch, a convert to Judaism. They presented these men to the apostles who prayed and laid hands on them. The word of God continued to spread, and the number of the disciples in Jerusalem increased greatly; even a large group of priests were becoming obedient to the faith.

∧

The Acts of the Apostles offers a realistic account of both the wonders and the struggles of the early Church. In addition to being a learning, loving, worshiping, and evangelizing community, the Church also experienced both internal and external difficulties, especially as it continued to grow. We might expect that this community of faith, living in the light of the resurrection and blessed with the Holy Spirit, was free from rivalries and prejudices. Yet as the numbers increased, the tensions also grew. Acts shows us how the community dealt with these challenges and found resolutions that serve as models for the Church in every age.

Among the Jewish disciples of Jesus, there were Hellenists, who spoke Greek and favored greater assimilation of the Jewish culture with the others, and Hebrews, who favored sharper separation and national identity in language and culture. Consciousness of this distinction led to suspicions of unfair discrimination, a situation that many multicultural communities experience in some form. In this text, Hellenists complain that their widows are being neglected by the Hebrews in the daily distribution of food and clothing for those in need.

The way the Church solved this difficulty is an example for resolving similar challenges in the Church today. The Twelve acted collegially, discerning together and gathering the community to outline the problem. Following the principle of subsidiarity—allowing the task to be performed at the lowest appropriate level—they requested that the Hellenist community choose seven men to serve them in the daily task of distributing goods. These were to be chosen because of their evident goodness and integrity, "filled with the Spirit and wisdom" (Acts 6:3). By appointing these men to service through formal prayer and the laying on of hands, the apostles could continue their task of serving the whole community by leading prayer and engaging in the ministry of the word.

By wisely resolving this difficulty, the unity of the Church was restored. Because the community reached inwardly to resolve the crisis, its outreach flourished and its numbers greatly increased.

JOHN 14:1-12

Jesus said to his disciples: "Do not let your hearts be troubled. You have faith in God; have faith also in me. In my Father's house there are many dwelling places. If there were not, would I have told you that I am going to prepare a place for you? And if I go and prepare a place for you, I will come back again and take you to myself, so that where I am you also may be. Where I am going you know the way." Thomas said to him, "Master, we do not know where you are going; how can we know the way?" Jesus said to him, "I am the way and the truth and the life. No one comes to the Father except through me. If you know me, then you will also know my Father. From now on you do know him and have seen him." Philip said to him, "Master, show us the Father, and that will be enough for us." Jesus said to him, "Have I been with you for so long a time and you still do not know me, Philip? Whoever has seen me has seen the Father. How can you say, 'Show us the Father'? Do you not believe that I am in the Father and the Father is in me? The words that I speak to you I do not speak on my own. The Father who dwells in me is doing his works. Believe me that I am in the Father and the Father is in me, or else, believe because of the works themselves. Amen, amen, I say to you, whoever believes in me will do the works that I do, and will do greater ones than these, because I am going to the Father."

The Danish philosopher Soren Kierkegaard said that life must be lived "forwards," but it can only be understood "backwards." This is how the early Church experienced its ongoing role in God's plan. While the community continued to grow, it looked back at the ancient Scriptures and the life of Jesus to understand more fully its own meaning and purpose. This is also why the Gospel readings of the remaining Sundays of Easter present the last discourse of Jesus before his passion. With Easter faith, the Church can listen anew to these treasured words of Jesus, recounted in the Gospel of John, the full significance of which is revealed only in the light of his resurrection.

There is a gentle urgency about the first words of this Gospel: "Do not let your hearts be troubled. You have faith in God; have faith also in me" (John 14:1). Having faith, in John's Gospel, is personal and relational. Jesus urges his disciples to place their trust in God and in himself, and to do all they can to overcome their fears and doubts with confidence and fidelity. Jesus consoles his disciples by assuring them that he will not forget them after his departure. In fact, he tells them that one of the purposes of his leaving is to prepare a place for them among the many dwelling places in the household of his Father. The image suggests abundant space, family closeness, and belonging among those who put their faith in Jesus. As Son of the Father, Jesus establishes his disciples as members of the Father's household and makes his own home a permanent, eternal residence for them.

When Thomas responds that the disciples do not know where Jesus is going or how to get there, Jesus assures them that they will not need to find their own way to the Father or to use their own resources for the journey. Jesus says, "I am the way and the truth and the life. No one comes to the Father except through me" (John 14:6), declaring that he himself is the road to the Father's house. He himself is the way to experience the very essence of truth and the fullness of life, the greatest aspirations of all people. Jesus is going to the Father, whose love defines the meaning of home; all the homes we have ever known in this life pale by comparison.

MEDITATIO

Ponder these inspired texts from the past with a view to understanding the present life we share in Christ and the future life we hope to attain.

- Diversity in membership brings tensions that can either push a community forward in a positive way or pull it apart in a negative way. What are some of the tensions involved in a multicultural Church? How does the Church today benefit from its diversity?

- The church in Jerusalem wisely responded to its inner problems, and as a result, its outreach flourished and its numbers grew. What can the Church today learn in this regard from the Church in its infancy?

- How do you experience Kierkegaard's maxim that life must be lived "forwards" and understood "backwards" in your life with Christ?

- What aspects of being home do you most enjoy? Jesus says that there are many dwelling places in his Father's house and that he is going to prepare a place for you. What do you look forward to the most when you consider dwelling in the Father's house?

- Thomas expresses the question that haunts us all: "How can we know the way?" (John 14:5). In response, we are offered not a map but a person—Jesus Christ. What are the implications of Jesus' words for your own life: "I am the way and the truth and the life" (14:6)?

ORATIO

After you've listened to what God has to say to you through these Scriptures, consider what you want to say to God in response. You might want to begin with these words:

Son of the Father, you are the way and the truth and the life. Show me the way that leads to the eternal home where you live with the Father. Teach me the truth that overcomes my doubts. Fill me with the fullness of life that lasts forever.

Continue responding to God in prayer in the words that arise from your own experience with the Scriptures.

CONTEMPLATIO

When the words of prayer are no longer necessary or helpful, just rest silently and confidently in the One who is the way and the truth and the life. Trust that he will guide you into the future.

OPERATIO

Before his departure from his disciples, Jesus said, "Whoever believes in me will do the works that I do, and will do greater ones than these, because I am going to the Father" (John 14:12). What are some of these greater works of the Church? How can you participate in these greater works because the risen Lord reigns in your life?

Sixth Sunday of Easter

LECTIO

⋏

Place before you a cross, icon, candle, or some other symbol of the risen Christ as you read the texts to enhance your awareness that all Scripture is Christ-centered. Ask the Holy Spirit to help you listen and respond to the *sacra pagina* as you reflect on the texts of this Easter liturgy.

When you have quieted your external and internal distractions, dedicate this time for sacred conversation with God.

ACTS 8:5-8, 14-17

Philip went down to the city of Samaria and proclaimed the Christ to them. With one accord, the crowds paid attention to what was said by Philip when they heard it and saw the signs he was doing. For unclean spirits, crying out in a loud voice, came out of many possessed people, and many paralyzed or crippled people were cured. There was great joy in that city.

Now when the apostles in Jerusalem heard that Samaria had accepted the word of God, they sent them Peter and John, who went down and prayed for them, that they might receive the Holy Spirit, for it had not yet fallen upon any of them; they had only been baptized in the name of the Lord Jesus. Then they laid hands on them and they received the Holy Spirit.

⋏

The liturgy of this Sunday of Easter directs our attention to the Holy Spirit as the parting gift of the risen Jesus. In John's Gospel, Jesus promises to send the Spirit to remain with his disciples after his departure, and the Acts of the Apostles demonstrates the work of the Holy Spirit within the expanding Church. In this passage, the gospel message moves beyond Jerusalem and into the region of Samaria. The Spirit empowers Philip to do among the Samaritans what Jesus did during his own ministry. He proclaims the good news and performs wonderful works among the people.

In going to the Samaritans, Philip is reaching out to the margins because the Samaritans were held in contempt by the Jews in Jerusalem. He is continuing a mission begun by Jesus, when he encountered the Samaritan woman at a well and she brought her townspeople to believe in him as Savior of the world (John 4-42). Philip's intrepid venture among a people previously thought to be enemies is impelled and guided by the Holy Spirit. Through Philip's ministry, the Samaritans at last hear of the resurrection of Jesus, and they are baptized in his name.

The Church's understanding of the boundaries of God's people is changing rapidly. No one would ever have thought that the Samaritans would become disciples of the Jewish Messiah. Acts challenges readers to consider how many other people who are perceived as distant from God will receive the gospel of Christ.

In order to demonstrate the continuity between the work of the first missionaries and the ministry of the apostles in Jerusalem, Peter and John are sent to confirm the faith and baptisms of these new Christians. The apostles' prayers and the laying on of hands provide a physical and sacramental link between the apostles and the work of the expanding Church. They embrace the Samaritans as brothers and sisters in the newly expanding family of God made known in the resurrection of Jesus. The Samaritans receive the Holy Spirit, and so they share with the other disciples in the joy, courage, confidence, and self-dedication that mark those anointed by the Spirit.

JOHN 14:15-21

Jesus said to his disciples: "If you love me, you will keep my commandments. And I will ask the Father, and he will give you another Advocate to be with you always, the Spirit of truth, whom the world cannot accept, because it neither sees nor knows him. But you know him, because he remains with you, and will be in you. I will not leave you orphans; I will come to you. In a little while the world will no longer see me, but you will see me, because I live and you will live. On that day you will realize that I am in my Father and you are in me and I in you. Whoever has my commandments and observes them is the one who loves me. And whoever loves me will be loved by my Father, and I will love him and reveal myself to him."

Λ

This passage from Jesus' final discourse to his disciples begins and ends with love. In between is Jesus' promise of the Holy Spirit, who will unite the disciples to Jesus, as Jesus is united with the Father. This wonderful flow of love created through the Spirit is the font of the Church's life and the source of all the Church's gifts.

If the disciples love Jesus and remain in union with him, then this communion will provide the divine energy to follow Jesus' commands to love God and love others. The ability to love as Jesus loved is rooted in the disciples' love of Jesus, who pours forth divine love into their lives. And the more the disciples act out of the love of Christ, the more deeply they experience that love, the love with which the Father has loved the Son.

This love between Jesus and his disciples is made possible through the Holy Spirit, whom Jesus calls the "Advocate" and the "Spirit of truth" (John 14:16, 17). The word translated as "Advocate" comes from the Greek word "Paraclete," which literally means "one called to the side of another." "Paraclete" can also be translated as "Helper," "Counselor," or "Comforter." The Holy Spirit will do for the disciples what Jesus himself did for them when he was living in their midst—especially encouraging and teaching them. The Spirit of truth will assist believers in discovering all the real and practical implications of the truth revealed by Jesus.

Jesus assures his disciples he will not leave them orphaned. His impending departure will not leave them bereft of his love. They will not be homeless and will not need to be cared for by strangers. He is going to leave them in one way and remain with them in another way. His departure will not be a loss but will enable a different form of presence. The disciples will experience the Holy Spirit as an abiding presence. As Jesus tells his disciples, the Spirit "remains with you, and will be in you" (John 14:17). It is the presence of the Holy Spirit that empowers the divine dwelling of the Father and Jesus within the disciples. With the Spirit, Jesus says, "You will realize that I am in my Father and you are in me and I in you" (14:20).

MEDITATIO

The presence of the Holy Spirit enables God's word to dwell within you. Seek to assimilate these texts in all their depth so that you can respond to them with your life.

- Philip's ministry in Samaria indicates how the Holy Spirit impels the Church outward, breaking down previously held boundaries. How might the Church follow this same impulse of the Spirit today?

- After the Samaritans had received the word of God and were baptized, Peter and John invoked the Holy Spirit upon them through prayer and the laying on of hands. What sacramental traditions of the Church are emphasized in this encounter?

- Jesus spends much of his final discourse preparing his followers for life in the age of the Spirit. What are some of the changes Jesus emphasizes for the Church after his departure? If you were one of the apostles, what thoughts and feelings might you have experienced as you listened to him?

- Jesus says that the world cannot accept, see, or know the Holy Spirit. The divine life of the Spirit is simply impossible to experience for those who contact reality only through the physical senses. How do you experience the presence of God's Spirit in your own life?

- The word Jesus used for his abiding Spirit with his disciples can be translated as "Advocate," "Helper," "Counselor," or "Comforter." How has reading the inspired Scriptures helped you to experience the presence of the Spirit in these ways?

ORATIO

After reflecting on the meaning of these texts, respond with praise, thanksgiving, and petition:

Risen Lord, send forth your Holy Spirit upon us to be our Advocate, Helper, Counselor, and Comforter. Give me your Spirit of truth to guide me as I read the inspired Scriptures and continue your revealing work within me.

Continue praying in praise of Christ's risen glory, in petition for the understanding to know the truth, and in thanksgiving for the insights you have received.

CONTEMPLATIO

Jesus said, "You will realize that I am in my Father and you are in me and I in you" (John 14:20). Rest in God's love, knowing that the Holy Spirit enables you to enter into the divine love flowing between the Father and the Son.

OPERATIO

The Holy Spirit impelled Philip and the early Church outward, breaking boundaries that defined God's people. The Spirit continues to thrust us out of our comfortable nests and into new missions, knowing that we will never be orphaned or abandoned. How can I respond to the Holy Spirit nudging me outward?

The Ascension of the Lord

LECTIO

ʌ

Approach these texts with expectant faith, trusting that God wishes to transform your heart with the power of his word. Read these texts aloud, seeking to hear God's word within them, without any presumptions. Listen to them in a new way, guided by God's renewing Spirit.

ACTS 1:1-11

In the first book, Theophilus, I dealt with all that Jesus did and taught until the day he was taken up, after giving instructions through the Holy Spirit to the apostles whom he had chosen. He presented himself alive to them by many proofs after he had suffered, appearing to them during forty days and speaking about the kingdom of God. While meeting with them, he enjoined them not to depart from Jerusalem, but to wait for "the promise of the Father about which you have heard me speak; for John baptized with water, but in a few days you will be baptized with the Holy Spirit."

When they had gathered together they asked him, "Lord, are you at this time going to restore the kingdom to Israel?" He answered them, "It is not for you to know the times or seasons that the Father has established by his own authority. But you will receive power when the Holy Spirit comes upon you, and you will be my witnesses in Jerusalem, throughout

Judea and Samaria, and to the ends of the earth." When he had said this, as they were looking on, he was lifted up, and a cloud took him from their sight. While they were looking intently at the sky as he was going, suddenly two men dressed in white garments stood beside them. They said, "Men of Galilee, why are you standing there looking at the sky? This Jesus who has been taken up from you into heaven will return in the same way as you have seen him going into heaven."

The readings for the Ascension of the Lord connect Jesus with his Church, which is the very purpose of the Acts of the Apostles. As Luke begins this book, he links what has already been told about Jesus' life, death, and resurrection to his ongoing account of the Church's early history. We are told that the risen Jesus gave ample proof of his resurrection by appearing to his apostles and teaching them over a period of forty days. We also know that Jesus instructed them to wait in Jerusalem for "the promise of the Father" (Acts 1:4), their baptism with the Holy Spirit.

The "forty days" of Jesus' appearances to his apostles is reminiscent of Moses' forty days on Mount Sinai, Elijah's forty-day sojourn on that same mountain, and the forty years of Israel's wandering in the wilderness while God taught them to be his people. Each of these "forty" experiences is a transition to a new experience of God. Jesus' ascension, after giving the apostles forty days of Easter manifestations, expresses a new aspect of the Easter mystery. His return to the Father means that Jesus will live in the power of his risen glory at the Father's side and that he will share his power with his Church through the promised Holy Spirit.

Gathering with Jesus, the apostles ask him, "Lord, are you at this time going to restore the kingdom to Israel?" (Acts 1:6). They seem to hope that the work of ending injustices and witnessing to God's kingdom can all be done for them without too much collaboration on their own part. While Jesus does not directly answer their question, he points them to the coming of the Holy Spirit, who will empower them to be witnesses of the gospel "in Jerusalem, throughout Judea and Samaria, and to the ends of the earth" (1:8).

MATTHEW 28:16-20

The eleven disciples went to Galilee, to the mountain to which Jesus had ordered them. When they saw him, they worshiped, but they doubted. Then Jesus approached and said to them, "All power in heaven and on earth has been given to me. Go, therefore, and make disciples of all nations, baptizing them in the name of the Father, and of the Son, and of the Holy Spirit, teaching them to observe all that I have commanded you. And behold, I am with you always, until the end of the age."

Like the beginning of Acts, the concluding verses of Matthew's Gospel also connect Jesus with his Church. The ongoing memory, motivating power, divine presence, and sacramental life of Jesus are still present in the world after two millennia because of his Church. The Gospel demonstrates this connection of Jesus with his Church in two ways: first, by specifying a threefold mission for the disciples and, second, by assuring them of Jesus' continual presence.

The final moments of the Gospel take place on a majestic mountain in Galilee. After the long and painful ministry with Jesus that ended on a cross in Jerusalem, the risen Lord calls his disciples back to Galilee, the place of their first calling and first mission. As we enter the Gospel scene, we, too, are called again to discipleship, to new responsibilities, to the task of being the Church. In Matthew's Gospel, mountains are places of teaching and transfiguration. Here on this mountain in Galilee, Jesus gives his final teaching, and his disciples are transfigured into evangelizers, baptizers, and teachers in his Church.

The commissioning of the disciples reflects the threefold mission that Jesus gives to his Church. The initial task is the proclamation of the good news. When new disciples receive the word, they are brought into the life of the Church through baptism. Then ongoing teaching in the way of Jesus must form and guide new disciples. The central responsibility of disciples is to make more disciples through evangelization, baptism, and teaching.

When the disciples saw the risen Lord on the mountain, "they worshiped, but they doubted" (Matthew 28:17). This post-resurrection mixture of faith and doubt is not so much disbelief as it is hesitation to accept Christ's call and its responsibilities; the disciples know only too well their own weaknesses. But the mission of the Church is possible only because of the promise of the risen Lord: "I am with you always, until the end of the age" (28:20). Though the responsibilities of disciples are daunting, the resources available to them in Jesus' authority and presence are more than adequate for the task. The disciples will experience his abiding presence in his Church through the same Spirit that empowered Jesus during his public life. This presence of Jesus gives confidence to disciples in every age, guiding and confirming their decisions and actions, as they await his coming again.

MEDITATIO

Ascension challenges us to ponder the absence of Jesus' physical presence and his new and abiding presence within his Church. Consider how these Scripture passages encourage you to respond to the final mandates of Jesus.

- For the first forty days of the Easter season, Jesus appeared to his followers and spoke to them about the kingdom of God. How has the Lord been working in your life during these weeks of Easter? How have these days marked a transition to a new experience of God for you?

- As a cloud took Jesus from the sight of his apostles, they remained looking intently at the sky. Some people continue to allow Christianity to degenerate into sky-gazing; meanwhile, the world waits for witnesses to the gospel. What is the mission Jesus has given to his Church?

- The risen Lord has commissioned his Church to a world-wide mission. In Acts, Jesus tells his disciples that they will be his witnesses "to the ends of the earth" (1:8). In Matthew's Gospel, he commands them to "make disciples

of all nations" (28:19). How can the Church better cultivate an awareness of its worldwide mission in its members?

- Jesus commissions his disciples to make more disciples
  through evangelization, baptism, and teaching. In what
  ways do you help carry out this mission of the Church
  today?

- The readings for this feast of the Ascension connect Jesus
  with his Church. Acts tells us that Jesus assured the Church
  of the indwelling power of the Holy Spirit (1:8). Matthew's
  Gospel assures us that Jesus will be with us always (28:20).
  How do these promises give you confidence as a disciple
  today? In what ways do you experience the continuing
  presence of Jesus through his Spirit in the Church?

ORATIO

You have listened and reflected on the call of the risen Lord to
his disciples through these Scriptures. Now vocalize your response
to his call in prayer:

Lord, all power in heaven and on earth has been given to
you by the Father. Give me the desire to worship you and the
courage to be a witness to the good news you have brought to
the world. Help me to do your will on earth as it is in heaven
until you come in glory.
Continue praying in your own words, using some of the

thoughts, words, and images from the Scriptures.

CONTEMPLATIO

⅄

Jesus has assured you, "I am with you always" (Matthew 28:20). Slowly repeat these comforting and assuring words as you rest in the presence of the risen Lord, worshiping him with silent praise.

OPERATIO

⅄

The resurrected Jesus ordered his disciples to return to Galilee to meet him there. Where did you experience your first calling or mission from Jesus? What can you do to recover the freshness and enthusiasm of that initial realization?

Seventh Sunday of Easter

LECTIO

⅄

Between Ascension and Pentecost, the liturgy focuses on Jesus' empowerment of his disciples. During these final days of the Easter season, ponder the mission you have received from Jesus as he reigns over the Church from the Father's side.

Read these texts aloud, seeking to hear God's word within them. Listen to them in a new way, without any presumptions, guided by God's renewing Spirit.

ACTS 1:12-14

After Jesus had been taken up to heaven the apostles returned to Jerusalem from the mount called Olivet, which is near Jerusalem, a sabbath day's journey away.

When they entered the city they went to the upper room where they were staying, Peter and John and James and Andrew, Philip and Thomas, Bartholomew and Matthew, James son of Alphaeus, Simon the Zealot, and Judas son of James. All these devoted themselves with one accord to prayer, together with some women, and Mary the mother of Jesus, and his brothers.

⅄

Luke's account picks up the story of the apostles immediately after they have experienced the Ascension of Jesus. They have been left, but they have been left with a mission to accomplish: they are to be witnesses of Jesus, beginning in Jerusalem and continuing in an ever-expanding mission to the ends of the earth. Yet first they have been told to wait for the promise of the Father, the power of the Holy Spirit coming upon them.

The apostles travel the short distance over the steep descent from Mount Olivet and the equally steep ascent back into the city of Jerusalem. They return to the upper room where they had shared in the last supper of Jesus. Those gathered there had experienced the entire ministry of Jesus, including his crucifixion and his resurrection appearances. The eleven apostles are joined by Mary, the mother of Jesus, some of the women who had followed Jesus from Galilee, and some of Jesus' extended family. This is the nucleus of the Church that will be empowered for mission by the Father's gift. They gather in expectant prayer, waiting with trust for the descent of the Holy Spirit upon them.

This beginning of the second volume of Luke's writing mirrors the beginning of his first volume, the Gospel of Luke. He begins his Gospel with the coming of the Holy Spirit upon Mary, the mother of Jesus, in order to give birth to Israel's Savior. Luke begins Acts with the coming of the Holy Spirit upon Mary, the mother of Jesus, and the apostles in order to give birth to the Church. As with Jesus, who was filled with the Holy Spirit throughout his saving mission on earth, the Church will be filled with the Holy Spirit for its expanding mission in the world.

JOHN 17:1-11A

Jesus raised his eyes to heaven and said, "Father, the hour has come. Give glory to your son, so that your son may glorify you, just as you gave him authority over all people, so that your son may give eternal life to all you gave him. Now this is eternal life, that they should know you, the only true God, and the one whom you sent, Jesus Christ. I glorified you on earth by accomplishing the work that you gave me to do. Now glorify me, Father, with you, with the glory that I had with you before the world began.

"I revealed your name to those whom you gave me out of the world. They belonged to you, and you gave them to me, and they have kept your word. Now they know that everything you gave me is from you, because the words you gave to me I have given to them, and they accepted them and truly understood that I came from you, and they have believed that you sent me. I pray for them. I do not pray for the world but for the ones you have given me, because they are yours, and everything of mine is yours and everything of yours is mine, and I have been glorified in them. And now I will no longer be in the world, but they are in the world, while I am coming to you."

This passage from John's Gospel continues the last discourse of Jesus, but here Jesus turns from addressing his disciples and raises his eyes heavenward to pray to his Father. Of course, Jesus wants his disciples to eavesdrop on this intimate conversation because

Jesus is praying for them, and the Evangelist wants his readers to listen in because Jesus is praying for them and for all of us. He prays that the Father will protect and guide us during our sojourn in the world.

The scope of Jesus' prayer extends from the time before the world existed, when he was in the presence of the Father, to the complete accomplishment of his mission on earth. Addressing his Father, Jesus prays, "Give glory to your son, so that your son may glorify you" (John 17:1). In the Bible, giving glory to another means externally manifesting a person's deeper hidden nature. Jesus gives glory to the Father through manifesting his love to the whole world, accomplishing the work the Father gave him to do. Jesus' deepest nature is his glory as the eternal Word of God, the glory he had in the Father's presence before his mission on earth. Jesus desires to return to that glory, but he desires to take us with him.

The purpose of Jesus' mission is to give us "eternal life" (John 17:2). The new characteristic of this life is not just the fact that it lasts forever; even more important is that it is a new quality of life for the believer. Eternal life is God's own life, a life that he wants us to share because he loves us so much. Jesus describes this life as knowing the Father and the Son. This knowing is a personal, experiential union with God, an experience that is entered through the gift of faith when we surrender to God's incomparable love.

As Jesus' earthly ministry is ending and he is about to return to the glory he had from eternity with the Father, he points to his fragile group of disciples. He prays for them because they will remain in the world. Jesus has been glorified in them because they have received and believed the revelation he has given them from the

90

Father. He will be glorified in them as they continue expressing in the world the same quality of love that Jesus has shown in the gift of himself for all. Though Jesus' mission in the world is coming to an end, his disciples will continue as the bearers of his ongoing mission in the world.

MEDITATIO

The Scriptures focus on the prayer of Mary and the apostles as they await the coming of the Holy Spirit and on the prayer of Jesus as he prepares to return to the Father. Ponder your own prayer and the mission that it empowers.

- Luke parallels the beginning of his Gospel and the beginning of Acts. What message might Luke want to communicate about the Church and its mission in the world?

- As Jesus departed from his disciples to return to the Father, he left them with a mission. But before the disciples proclaimed the gospel, they went to the upper room and devoted themselves to prayer. What does this scene teach you about the importance of prayer for the Church and for your own life?

- According to the prayer of Jesus, this is eternal life: "that they should know you, the only true God, and the one whom you sent, Jesus Christ" (John 17:3). In what sense is eternal life a sharing in the life of God?

- As he prepared to return to the glory of his Father, Jesus prayed for you. He asked that the Father protect you and guide you during your sojourn in the world. What else might Jesus have prayed for while thinking of you?

- Jesus prays to the Father: "Give glory to your son, so that your son may glorify you" (John 17:1). How does Jesus glorify the Father? How do you glorify Jesus by your life?

ORATIO

Imaginatively respond to these Scriptures in prayer, along with Mary, the mother of Jesus, the apostles, and the other disciples gathered in the upper room. You may begin with these words:

Eternal Word of God, you have revealed the true nature and love of the Father to us through your life, death, and resurrection. Help me to experience union with you and with the Father as I long to share eternal life more completely and more deeply.

Continue praying from your heart as if you were in the upper room.

CONTEMPLATIO

Continue to imagine that you are with the apostles, Mary, and the other relatives and disciples of Jesus. Rest in the company of these saints and martyrs, and know that they care for you. Ask this heavenly company to pray for you, and trust that God hears the prayers that they are offering for you.

OPERATIO

We are the ongoing bearers of Christ's mission in the world. How can you learn to pray for the Church's mission and for your own mission in the world? Invoke the intercession of the saints of heaven as you pray this week.

Pentecost Sunday

LECTIO

As you prepare to hear the Scriptures for the feast of Pentecost, become aware of the rhythm of your breathing. Breathe in, being filled with the presence of God's Spirit. Breathe out, letting go of your preoccupations and anxieties.

Listen for God's word to you within these sacred texts. Let God's renewing Spirit guide you to hear these Scriptures in a new way.

ACTS 2:1-11

When the time for Pentecost was fulfilled, they were all in one place together. And suddenly there came from the sky a noise like a strong driving wind, and it filled the entire house in which they were. Then there appeared to them tongues as of fire, which parted and came to rest on each one of them. And they were all filled with the Holy Spirit and began to speak in different tongues, as the Spirit enabled them to proclaim.

Now there were devout Jews from every nation under heaven staying in Jerusalem. At this sound, they gathered in a large crowd, but they were confused because each one heard them speaking in his own language. They were astounded, and in amazement they asked, "Are not all these people who are speaking Galileans? Then how does each of us hear them in his native language? We are Parthians, Medes, and Elamites, inhabitants of Mesopotamia, Judea and Cappadocia,

Pontus and Asia, Phrygia and Pamphylia, Egypt and the districts of Libya near Cyrene, as well as travelers from Rome, both Jews and converts to Judaism, Cretans and Arabs, yet we hear them speaking in our own tongues of the mighty acts of God."

⅄

The word "Pentecost" derives from the Greek word for "fiftieth." It marks fifty days after Passover on the Jewish calendar and fifty days after Easter on the Christian calendar. Among Jews it is known as "Shavuot" and celebrates the giving of the Law to Moses on Mount Sinai. For Christians it commemorates the coming of the Holy Spirit upon Jesus' disciples gathered in Jerusalem after his ascension.

As the disciples of Jesus are gathered with Mary and the twelve apostles, the house is filled with the sound of a mighty wind, and flames of fire descend and rest on each of them. The wind and the fire express the divine presence. They are outward signs and sacramental manifestations of an inner reality: "They were all filled with the Holy Spirit" (Acts 2:4). The fiery "tongues" become the gift of "different tongues" as the disciples begin to announce the good news of salvation "as the Spirit enabled them to proclaim" (2:3, 4). They are able to speak in a way that those present from all over the world can understand them in their own native language.

The event of Pentecost begs to be compared with the story of the Tower of Babel in the Book of Genesis. At Babel, in judgment for the sinful striving of men to defy God, the one language of humanity became confused so that they could no longer communicate. At Pentecost, the one gospel begins to be heard and understood in the languages of "every nation under heaven" (2:5). At Babel, men were climbing upward to usurp divine power; at Pentecost, God's power descends upon the disciples, restoring their ability to communicate across all the barriers that have been created by a sinful history. God is reuniting the human race in Christ by the power of the Holy Spirit.

JOHN 20:19-23

On the evening of that first day of the week, when the doors were locked, where the disciples were, for fear of the Jews, Jesus came and stood in their midst and said to them, "Peace be with you." When he had said this, he showed them his hands and his side. The disciples rejoiced when they saw the Lord. Jesus said to them again, "Peace be with you. As the Father has sent me, so I send you." And when he had said this, he breathed on them and said to them, "Receive the Holy Spirit. Whose sins you forgive are forgiven them, and whose sins you retain are retained."

The mandate that the risen Jesus gives his disciples at his appearance is a summary of his own life and the life of the Church: "As the Father has sent me, so I send you" (John 20:21). Jesus has revealed the Father for all to see—through his teachings, his healing signs, and finally through his total sacrifice on the cross. Now Jesus sends his disciples on that same mission. We are to be for the world what Jesus has been for the world. We are to embody the

Father's love, to teach and to heal, to comfort and bring peace, to love as Jesus loved.

Jesus enlivens and empowers his disciples as he breathes on them and says, "Receive the Holy Spirit" (John 20:22). As the Creator breathed life into the first human being (Genesis 2:7), Jesus breathes his Spirit into God's new creation, the community of disciples sent out to forgive, heal, teach, and love. The Spirit is the ongoing presence of Christ, continuing Christ's mission in the world in every age.

The biblical name for "Spirit" in Hebrew is *ruach*, a word which can mean either "wind" or "breath," in addition to "Spirit." The Greek word, *pneuma*, also expresses the multiple sense of wind, breath, and Spirit. The wind, on the one hand, is a sweeping force that cannot be contained, and thus, the image of the wind expresses the power, freedom, and transcendence of God's Spirit. Breath, on the other hand, is what is most intimate, inward, and personal, so the image of breath conveys the gentleness, peacefulness, and immanence of the Spirit.

In the first reading of Pentecost from Acts, the divine Spirit is manifested with a strong rushing wind. In the Gospel, Jesus' breath communicates the Spirit to his disciples. The Holy Spirit personifies this mystery of God's presence, which is both awesome power and overwhelming tenderness, a divine presence that inspires in people both reverent fear and irresistible attraction.

MEDITATIO

⅄

Ponder these Spirit-inspired Scriptures in the context of the Spirit-guided Church. Consider how God is leading you to a deeper understanding of your faith within the circumstances of your life.

- In Acts, the presence of the Holy Spirit is communicated through wind and fire, and in John's Gospel, the Spirit is given through the breath of Jesus. Why does God choose to reveal the Spirit's presence and power through the natural elements of the created world? Through what natural and sacramental symbols do you experience the Holy Spirit?

- Pentecost reminds us that we are people filled with the Spirit, people with gifts that the world desperately needs: wisdom for a world searching for meaning; knowledge for a world seeking insight; healing for a world torn apart by violence; prophecy for a world in need of direction; discernment for a world confronted by competing forces. What gifts of the Spirit have been given to you for the service of others? How do you engage these gifts for the benefit of others?

- The Hebrew and Greek words for "Spirit" also mean "wind" or "breath." In what sense are these two meanings different but complementary aspects of the Spirit's presence?

- Through the Holy Spirit, the disciples in Jerusalem were able to communicate the gospel in ways that all people could understand. The Spirit still enables people to hear one another across boundaries of differences in ways that deepen understanding. Why is this a critical aspect of the Spirit's work today?

- The power of the Holy Spirit worked wonders in and through the lives of the first disciples. That same Spirit has worked wonders in and through the lives of believers down through the ages. What wonders is the Spirit working in and through believers today? What might the Spirit be urging you to do?

ORATIO

After you've listened to what God has to say to you through these Scriptures, consider what you want to say to God in response. You might want to begin with these words:

Come, Holy Spirit, take away my timid and cowardly spirit, and give me a spirit of courage and fervor. Sanctify my heart for the glory of God's kingdom, and kindle in me the fire of your divine love.

Continue responding to God in prayer in the words that arise from your own experience of the Holy Spirit.

CONTEMPLATIO

⌒

Imagining the Holy Spirit as either wind or breath, let the Spirit fill you with grace and divine love. Trust that God's Spirit is recreating you from the inside out.

OPERATIO

⌒

At Pentecost, the Spirit of God took hold of the first disciples with a force like a mighty wind, and they were set on fire with zeal for the reign of God. As baptized and confirmed Christians, we, too, have been seized by that same Spirit; we, too, have been given gifts meant for the service of others. How can I stir up the grace of my baptism and confirmation as I continue to live in the Holy Spirit?

Chapter Four

Lectio Divina for the Easter Season: Year B

Easter Sunday of the Resurrection of the Lord

LECTIO

Quiet your inner spirit and free yourself from the distractions of the day so that you can hear the word of God. Kiss the text, or place your palms upon it as a sign of your reverence for Sacred Scripture and your desire to receive its transforming message.

Begin reading when you feel ready to hear God's voice. Read this familiar text as if for the first time, trying not to bring your own presumptions to the text, but instead, listening as if God is speaking to you anew.

ACTS 10:34A, 37-43

Peter proceeded to speak and said: "You know what has happened all over Judea, beginning in Galilee after the baptism that John preached, how God anointed Jesus of Nazareth with the Holy Spirit and power. He went about doing good and healing all those oppressed by the devil, for God was with him. We are witnesses of all that he did both in the country of the Jews and in Jerusalem. They put him to death by hanging him on a tree. This man God raised on the third day and granted that he be visible, not to all the people, but to us, the witnesses chosen by God in advance, who ate and drank with him after he rose from the dead. He commissioned us to preach to the people and testify that he is the one appointed by God as judge of the living and the dead. To him all the prophets bear witness, that everyone who believes in him will receive forgiveness of sins through his name."

⋏

The liturgy presents us with this sermon of Peter on Easter Sunday because it expresses the transforming joy of the resurrection of Jesus. After relating how Jesus' ministry led to his death on the cross, Peter reaches his climactic declaration about how God raised Jesus to life in fulfillment of God's prophetic promises of salvation. As a witness to this resurrection, God has sent Peter to testify "that everyone who believes in him will receive forgiveness of sins through his name" (Acts 10:43).

This sermon of Peter in the house of Cornelius offers a fine illustration of the process of Christian evangelization. First, we see that Peter offers witness to Jesus from his own experience. He speaks to his listeners about his own personal understanding of Jesus and his relationship with him. Second, Peter offers a simple but poignant message based on the life, death, and resurrection of Jesus himself. Third, Peter is compelled to witness because of his profound experience of being personally called to evangelize, since Jesus has commissioned him to preach the gospel. Fourth, Peter calls people to conversion when they are ready to hear the invitation. After helping the household to acknowledge their need for God's grace, he offers the means to salvation through faith in Jesus. And finally, Peter evangelizes with the conviction that all people are called by God to salvation. As a Jew speaking to a

Gentile audience, Peter knows that "everyone who believes" in Jesus will be drawn by God to new life (Acts 10:43).

Like all good preachers, Peter draws us into the drama. Like all who are baptized at Easter, we know that we have been offered forgiveness and a transformed life. We have heard the gospel of salvation, and we are called to receive the good news with an increasingly receptive heart. On this day of the Lord's resurrection, we know that we participate in the forgiveness and transformation offered through faith in the resurrected Lord.

After pausing to let the words of Peter sink in, begin reading the Gospel narrative of the resurrection. Read this familiar account as if for the first time, trusting that God will work deeply in your heart through the words of the Gospel according to Mark.

MARK 16:1-7*

When the sabbath was over, Mary Magdalene, Mary, the mother of James, and Salome bought spices so that they might go and anoint him. Very early when the sun had risen, on the first day of the week, they came to the tomb. They were saying to one another, "Who will roll back the stone for us from the entrance to the tomb?" When they looked up, they saw that the stone had been rolled back; it was very large. On entering the tomb they saw a young man sitting on the right side, clothed in a white robe, and they were utterly amazed. He said to them, "Do not be amazed! You seek Jesus of Nazareth, the crucified. He has been raised; he is not here. Behold

*This is the reading for the Easter Vigil Mass and an alternative reading for Easter Day. The reading for Easter Day is John 20:1-9.

the place where they laid him. But go and tell his disciples and Peter, 'He is going before you to Galilee; there you will see him, as he told you.'"

⋏

After the death and burial of Jesus, the hearts of the women of Galilee are as heavy as the stone rolled across the tomb, and their hopes are as dead as the tortured body placed within it. But very early on the first day of the new week, just as light begins to mingle with darkness and overcome it, they come to the tomb, wondering who will roll back the stone for them. Discovering that the stone has already been rolled away, they enter the tomb and find there a young messenger of God. The Easter message he proclaims to them means that the tomb of Jesus is no longer the place of death; it is the place of hope and renewal, of new life and resurrection. After assuring the women that Jesus has been raised, the angel gives them their mission: to go and witness to Peter and the other disciples that Jesus is going ahead of them to Galilee where they will see him.

The earliest manuscripts of Mark's Gospel do not contain any resurrection appearances of Jesus, as in the other three Gospels; the longer and shorter endings to his Gospel were added after his death (16:9-20). Most scholars admit that Mark intended to end his Gospel with the angel's commission to the women (16:7). Although Mark certainly knew the traditions in the Church of resurrection appearances, he wanted to leave his Gospel radically open-ended. Writing in Rome to teach people in the next generation how to be disciples, Mark wanted to assure his readers that resurrection is not the end of the gospel but only the beginning.

Our problem is that we have heard the story of Jesus so often that we fail to react because we think we know how it ends. But that is Mark's point: we don't know how it will end. Jesus has gone ahead of Peter and the other disciples to Galilee, the place where they first met Jesus and received their call. Mark doesn't tell us what happens next. The gospel continues and is completed only in the lives of those recreated by God in the light of the risen Christ. Like all disciples, we are invited to accept in faith the announcement of his resurrection and to continue the gospel in every age.

MEDITATIO

Consider what aspects of your life experiences are highlighted by the biblical texts. Allow the book of your life and the inspired Scriptures to dialogue so that you come to understand the significance of these readings for yourself during this Easter season.

- The sermon of Peter illustrates important aspects of Christian evangelization. What features of Peter's proclamation might be particularly helpful to you as you seek to share the good news with others?

- Peter numbers himself among the witnesses who "ate and drank" with Jesus after he rose from the dead (Acts 10:41). In what ways does the Church also eat and drink with the risen Christ? How does this union strengthen your faith in the resurrection?

- Jesus' crucifixion focuses on the deeds of men, as do so many of the bloody events of human history, but the resurrection highlights women, the bearers and protectors of life. Why do you think God entrusted the first proclamation of the resurrection to women?

- The angel's commission to the women to go and tell the disciples that the risen Jesus is going ahead of them to Galilee offers a fresh beginning to those who had fled in denial and desertion. In what ways does the resurrection offer you the hope of forgiveness and a new calling?

- The end of Mark's Gospel, with its abrupt ending, could rightly be called a cliffhanger. Why did later writers attempt to add a more "fitting" end to the Gospel? What was Mark's intention in ending his Gospel this way?

ORATIO

Pray to God in response to what you have discovered within yourself from your listening and reflection. You may begin with these words:

Risen Lord, you have defeated the power of sin with your sorrowful passion and the power of death with your glorious resurrection. Help me to trust in your victory, and teach me how to speak the good news with my lips and embody the gospel with my life.

Continue to interact with God as the One who knows

you intimately, cares about you deeply, and accepts you unconditionally.

CONTEMPLATIO

Imaginatively place yourself before the empty tomb of Christ. Let the emptiness of the tomb and the hope that fills the air refresh you. Rest with this image, and let it infuse you with trust and confidence in God.

OPERATIO

The ending of Mark's Gospel presents you with the challenge of continuing the gospel with your own life. What can you do this Easter season to renew your discipleship or learn to witness to the resurrection more effectively?

Second Sunday of Easter

LECTIO

Prepare your space for encountering God's word by lighting a candle or placing another visible symbol in front of you. Call upon the same Holy Spirit who inspired the sacred writers to fill your heart and kindle in you the fire of divine love.

As you read, highlight, underline, circle, or mark up the reading as a tool for interacting with the text. You will find that these marks help you be attentive to details and remember the words during your encounter with God's word.

ACTS 4:32-35

The community of believers was of one heart and mind, and no one claimed that any of his possessions was his own, but they had everything in common. With great power the apostles bore witness to the resurrection of the Lord Jesus, and great favor was accorded them all. There was no needy person among them, for those who owned property or houses would sell them, bring the proceeds of the sale, and put them at the feet of the apostles, and they were distributed to each according to need.

This summary of the communal life of the early Christians shows the practical outcomes of real faith in the resurrection. This faith in

Christ means that members of the Church have found the source of their joy and hope in the saving power of divine love. This implies that they no longer need to cling to status and possessions for their security. The description of the believers as being "of one heart and mind" (Acts 4:32) means that they seek genuine solidarity. They have compassion for one another and try to walk in the shoes of each other; they express a readiness to share their material resources so that no one is in need among them.

The communal life of the early Christians was not a kind of top-down socialism. Their giving was totally voluntary and sprang from an inner conviction of the worth of others and the desire to live in the power and grace of Christ's resurrection. Faith in the risen Christ is a totally transforming reality; it is a divine gift that first, changes the hearts and minds of the believers and, second, draws people together with a shared vision of life's meaning and purpose.

The apostles held a central role in the early Church. Their activity is expressed by two characteristics: "great power" and "great favor" (Acts 4:33). They bore witness to the resurrection through the strength that comes from God's grace. They were the overseers of the community and were at the center of its activity. Those who sold homes and property would put the proceeds "at the feet of the apostles" (4:35). The good of the whole community was represented by the apostles, and they oversaw the distribution of the community's resources. In all of this apostolic work, the Church bore practical witness to the resurrection.

JOHN 20:19-31

On the evening of that first day of the week, when the doors were locked, where the disciples were, for fear of the Jews, Jesus came and stood in their midst and said to them, "Peace be with you." When he had said this, he showed them his hands and his side. The disciples rejoiced when they saw the Lord. Jesus said to them again, "Peace be with you. As the Father has sent me, so I send you." And when he had said this, he breathed on them and said to them, "Receive the Holy Spirit. Whose sins you forgive are forgiven them, and whose sins you retain are retained."

Thomas, called Didymus, one of the Twelve, was not with them when Jesus came. So the other disciples said to him, "We have seen the Lord." But he said to them, "Unless I see the mark of the nails in his hands and put my finger into the nail-marks and put my hand into his side, I will not believe."

Now a week later his disciples were again inside and Thomas was with them. Jesus came, although the doors were locked, and stood in their midst and said, "Peace be with you." Then he said to Thomas, "Put your finger here and see my hands, and bring your hand and put it into my side, and do not be unbelieving, but believe." Thomas answered and said to him, "My Lord and my God!" Jesus said to him, "Have you come to believe because you have seen me? Blessed are those who have not seen and have believed."

Now Jesus did many other signs in the presence of his disciples that are not written in this book. But these are written that you may come to believe that Jesus is the Christ, the

Son of God, and that through this belief you may have life in his name.

⅄

The risen Jesus stands before his terrified and disillusioned disciples in all of his glorified humanity and shows them his wounds. He greets the disciples with "peace" (John 20:19) and displays his wounded hands and side as the way for them to know and believe in him. A risen Lord without his wounds would not have been believable to that wounded community in Jerusalem and would have little to say to our broken humanity today.

In inviting his disciples to accept the gift of peace, Jesus demonstrates that it is not a peace that ignores the brutality inflicted on him. It is a peace that recognizes full well the horror of what has occurred and results from a willingness to enter into the processes of forgiveness and healing. Jesus is able to show his wounds, not as something that needs to be avenged, but as something that has already begun to be reconciled through his Spirit. This peace enables the disciples to let their fear give way to joy.

Our own wounds express a great deal about who we are and the life we've lived. The death-camp number branded on a survivor of the Shoah, the hidden marks of domestic violence, the scars of lifesaving surgery, the unspoken wounds to our own hearts: much of our identity lies in our wounds. Sometimes we allow our life to drain from our wounds; at other times we grow to new life at these broken places.

When Jesus returns to the community the next Sunday, Thomas voices the doubts of those who need to see with their own eyes and touch with their own hands. The doubts of Thomas are not just a stubborn resistance to believe; instead, they express the necessity of every person to come to faith through a personal encounter with Christ. The testimony of others can lead us to Christ, but only a personal experience of him leads to genuine faith. When Thomas comes to recognize the figure before him as Jesus raised from the dead, he proclaims him as "my Lord and my God!" (John 20:28)—the fullest confession of Jesus' identity in the New Testament. So the path to Easter faith in this Gospel scene moves from the disciples' fear and despair, through confusion and recognition, to the gift of the Holy Spirit and Thomas's profession of faith.

MEDITATIO

These inspired texts from Acts and John's Gospel are presented in the liturgy so that we can learn from and imitate the apostolic community and the early Church. Ponder and reflect on their revealing power.

- The summary description of the early Christians in Acts shows the practical outcomes of faith in the resurrection. How would you describe the practical effects of Easter on your own life?

- Acts describes the community of believers as being "of one heart and mind" (4:32). How might the power of Jesus' resurrection more effectively shape life within your family, religious community, or parish?

- The Gospel also allows that there are different ways that people come to faith: some through seeing, some without. Both are blessed. What keeps you from believing, and what helps you to believe?

- The wounded risen Jesus and the wounded disciple, Thomas, stood before one another. Why was Thomas able to experience forgiveness and faith through the wounds of Jesus? Why might you be better able to experience God's love and healing through Jesus' wounds rather than your own wounds?

- Jesus offered his forgiveness and peace to the disciples as he bestowed upon them the Holy Spirit. Then Jesus gave them the mission to forgive and retain sins in his name and to work for peace and reconciliation in the world. What are some of the ways in which the risen Lord offers forgiveness and reconciliation through his Church?

ORATIO

Use the images and emotions from your lectio and meditatio as the foundation of your prayerful response to God. Imagine the gratitude and healing of the disciples as they encountered the risen Christ. You may begin your prayer with these words:

Wounded and risen Lord, you offer your healing peace and the gift of faith to disciples in every age. Empower me with the Holy Spirit, and send me to offer your healing, forgiveness, and reconciliation to others.

Continue voicing the prayer that issues from your heart as you ponder these scenes with gratitude.

CONTEMPLATIO

The Easter appearance narratives are filled with solemn awe, as the disciples were incapable of fully expressing what they were experiencing. As the words of your prayer become inadequate to express your heart, just remain in silence before the risen Lord, filled with joy and faith.

OPERATIO

The story is told of a man who dies and comes before God. "Where are your wounds?" asks God. "I have none," said the man. "Why?" responds God. "Was there nothing worth fighting for?"

How is your Christian faith changing what you consider worth fighting for and being wounded by?

Third Sunday of Easter

LECTIO

Call upon the Holy Spirit to guide your listening to these sacred texts and to open your heart as you read. Vocalize the words of the text so that you not only read with your eyes but hear with your ears. Listen for the word of the Lord.

ACTS 3:13-15, 17-19

Peter said to the people: "The God of Abraham, the God of Isaac, and the God of Jacob, the God of our fathers, has glorified his servant Jesus, whom you handed over and denied in Pilate's presence when he had decided to release him. You denied the Holy and Righteous One and asked that a murderer be released to you. The author of life you put to death, but God raised him from the dead; of this we are witnesses. Now I know, brothers, that you acted out of ignorance, just as your leaders did; but God has thus brought to fulfillment what he had announced beforehand through the mouth of all the prophets, that his Christ would suffer. Repent, therefore, and be converted, that your sins may be wiped away."

The speeches of various figures throughout Acts contain a summary of early Christian preaching and the essential elements of faith. This brief excerpt of Peter's address is no exception. Peter addresses a Jewish audience in the area of the Temple in Jerusalem, speaking to them about the God of Abraham, Isaac, and Jacob. Peter identifies himself as a member of God's people and a recipient of the promises of "the God of our fathers" (Acts 3:13) along with his audience. Peter wants to demonstrate that everything that God has done in his servant Jesus is the culmination of a long history of prophecy and expectation.

Proclaiming how Jesus is the fulfillment of ancient Scriptures, Peter testifies to the significance of Jesus' death and resurrection. Jesus is the Messiah who suffered for his people, the Christ who fulfilled what God "had announced beforehand through the mouth of all the prophets" (Acts 3:18). He is "the Holy and Righteous One" (3:14) who was rejected by those he came to save. Yet their tragic denial and handing over of Jesus to death was met by God's raising him from the dead.

Peter admits that the religious leaders and the people of Jerusalem "acted out of ignorance" (Acts 3:17). Yet ignorance does not leave them without responsibility. For this reason, Peter urges the crowd to repent and be converted. Their sin of not recognizing Jesus as the Messiah and of putting him to death can be forgiven. If they turn away from sin and toward God, their sins will be "wiped away" (3:19). He emphasizes life, not death; repentance, not blame. The forgiving power of God can raise anyone from the death of sin, just as he raised Jesus from the grave.

LUKE 24:35-48

The two disciples recounted what had taken place on the way, and how Jesus was made known to them in the breaking of bread.

While they were still speaking about this, he stood in their midst and said to them, "Peace be with you." But they were startled and terrified and thought that they were seeing a ghost. Then he said to them, "Why are you troubled? And why do questions arise in your hearts? Look at my hands and my feet, that it is I myself. Touch me and see, because a ghost does not have flesh and bones as you can see I have." And as he said this, he showed them his hands and his feet. While they were still incredulous for joy and were amazed, he asked them, "Have you anything here to eat?" They gave him a piece of baked fish; he took it and ate it in front of them.

He said to them, "These are my words that I spoke to you while I was still with you, that everything written about me in the law of Moses and in the prophets and psalms must be fulfilled." Then he opened their minds to understand the Scriptures. And he said to them, "Thus it is written that the Christ would suffer and rise from the dead on the third day and that repentance, for the forgiveness of sins, would be preached in his name to all the nations, beginning from Jerusalem. You are witnesses of these things."

Both the words of Peter in Acts and of Jesus in Luke's Gospel seek to show listeners that the ancient Scriptures of Israel announced the Messiah's suffering and resurrection. As the risen Lord appears to his disciples, he reaffirms what he said to them during his earthly ministry: "Everything written about me in the law of Moses and in the prophets and psalms must be fulfilled" (Luke 24:44). The Torah, the writings of the prophets, and the ancient prayer book of God's people all speak of God's saving plan for the world.

The risen Jesus opens the disciples' minds by opening the Scriptures to them. In light of the resurrection, the disciples are now able to understand how the entirety of the Old Testament teachings fit together as promised and are completed in the dying and rising of Jesus the Messiah. The first two elements of God's plan have been completed—"that the Christ would suffer and rise from the dead on the third day"—and the third and final element still remains to be carried out—"that repentance, for the forgiveness of sins, would be preached in his name to all the nations" (Luke 24:46, 47). This remaining element of God's plan will be carried out by the disciples as witnesses to Jesus the Messiah and Savior.

The resurrection of Jesus changes everything for the disciples. At first the disciples are startled, terrified, troubled, and disbelieving. Yet Jesus stands in their midst and says, "Peace be with you" (Luke 24:36). His greeting wishes for them a fullness and wholeness that is brought about by his victory over all sources of fear. After Jesus demonstrates that he is real, they become joyful and incredulous because it all seems just too good to be true. Jesus describes the disciples as "witnesses of these things" (24:48). As witnesses of the death and resurrection of Jesus in Jerusalem, the disciples will go out from Jerusalem as witnesses of his salvation to all the nations. This appearance of the risen Jesus at the end of

Luke's Gospel is the foundation of the disciples' witness, which is the subject of Luke's Acts of the Apostles.

MEDITATIO

⁘

Reflect on these texts so that they may become a means of self-examination and scrutiny for you during this season. Consider how you can allow the printed text to become the living word of our liberating God.

- Peter urged his listeners to respond with repentance and conversion to the good news he preached. Repentance means a change of mind, heart, and behavior. Conversion means turning back to God. Why are repentance and conversion necessary in order to experience the forgiveness that God offers us?

- Peter told the crowd to "repent, . . . and be converted, that your sins may be wiped away" (Acts 3:19). The Greek term for "wipe away" also means "erase" or "obliterate." The term refers to what happens to letters written in ink when papyri are soaked and washed. Do you believe that God wipes away your sins completely when you repent and turn to him?

- Jesus emphasizes his "flesh and bones" and his hands and feet (Luke 24:39), inviting the disciples to touch him in order to know that his body is real. Why was it important to the disciples, and why is it important to you, that the risen Lord is the man of Galilee?

- Jesus said, "Everything written about me in the law of Moses and in the prophets and psalms must be fulfilled" (Luke 24:44). What can the Torah, the writing of the prophets, and the Book of Psalms tell you about Jesus? Why is it so important to know the ancient Scriptures in order to truly know Jesus?

- The path of Peter moves from his cowardly betrayal of Jesus, to the experience of forgiveness from the risen Lord, to his bold preaching in Jerusalem. What has moved Peter from fear to witness? How does Jesus lead others to make this transition today?

ORATIO

Using the words, images, and emotions from the texts you have reflected upon, offer your response to God's word. You may begin your prayer with these words:

Risen Lord, help me to know that your presence is real as you make yourself known in word and sacrament and in the lives of your disciples today. Send your Holy Spirit upon me so that I may be filled with joy and empowered to be your witness.

Continue your prayer with words that convey the sentiments of your heart. Try to express your prayer with joyful confidence, trusting in the Lord who frees you from fear and disbelief.

CONTEMPLATIO

Peter describes Jesus as "the author of life" (Acts 3:15). By this title he portrays Jesus as the first of many destined for resurrected and everlasting life. Rest in this wondrous image of Jesus, and place your eternal hope in him.

OPERATIO

Peter spoke with such conviction because he knew that Jesus was alive and had turned the tide of human history. In what ways this week can you be a part of the Church's witness to Christ's resurrection?

Fourth Sunday of Easter

LECTIO

Λ

Prepare your space for encountering God's living word in Scripture. Light a candle, or place some other visible symbol before you to help you focus on the texts. Call upon the Holy Spirit to enlighten your eyes and your mind as you read the Sacred Scriptures.

Begin reading when you are prepared to encounter God through the words of the *sacra pagina*.

ACTS 4:8-12

Peter, filled with the Holy Spirit, said: "Leaders of the people and elders: If we are being examined today about a good deed done to a cripple, namely, by what means he was saved, then all of you and all the people of Israel should know that it was in the name of Jesus Christ the Nazorean whom you crucified, whom God raised from the dead; in his name this man stands before you healed. He is the stone rejected by you, the builders, which has become the cornerstone. There is no salvation through anyone else, nor is there any other name under heaven given to the human race by which we are to be saved."

Λ

The Book of Acts demonstrates that the ministry of Jesus continues in the community of apostles. The teaching, reconciling, and healing work of the risen Lord is extended into the life of the Church through the Holy Spirit. Peter's address to the religious leaders of Jerusalem was in response to the healing of a man who was lame from birth and begged for alms at the Temple gate. Peter offered him more than alms could buy; he gave him the ability to walk. The healing of the crippled beggar was not performed as a feat of magic to amaze the crowds but, like the miracles of Jesus, as a sign of God's saving presence in their midst. The man's walking, leaping, and praising God is a tangible sign of the wholeness that salvation brings and that God desires for all people.

Arrested and brought to trial before the religious leaders of Jerusalem, Peter addresses his examiners. He sees his judicial inquiry as an opportunity to proclaim the name of Jesus Christ to the leaders and the people they represent. Without apology, Peter declares what he has done and by whom it was made possible. At the center of his testimony, Peter proclaims the source of the healing: "All of you and all the people of Israel should know that it was in the name of Jesus Christ the Nazorean whom you crucified, whom God raised from the dead" (Acts 4:10). Peter speaks like a prophet and confronts his listeners with their own accountability. Jesus is the one whom they have crucified and whom God vindicated by raising him to life.

Peter uses the image of the discarded cornerstone to express the divine design of Jesus' rejection and vindication. The image comes from the psalms: "The stone which the builders rejected / has become the cornerstone" (Psalm 118:22). Jesus is that stone rejected by God's people but made the cornerstone of God's new temple. Jesus is now the source of salvation for all humanity. In his name, God offers healing and the fullness of life to all.

JOHN 10:11-18

Jesus said: "I am the good shepherd. A good shepherd lays down his life for the sheep. A hired man, who is not a shepherd and whose sheep are not his own, sees a wolf coming and leaves the sheep and runs away, and the wolf catches and scatters them. This is because he works for pay and has no concern for the sheep. I am the good shepherd, and I know mine and mine know me, just as the Father knows me and I know the Father; and I will lay down my life for the sheep. I have other sheep that do not belong to this fold. These also I must lead, and they will hear my voice, and there will be one flock, one shepherd. This is why the Father loves me, because I lay down my life in order to take it up again. No one takes it from me, but I lay it down on my own. I have power to lay it down, and power to take it up again. This command I have received from my Father."

⋏

The prophets presented the unfaithful leaders of Israel as bad shepherds, who scatter their flock and consign them to the wolves. In contrast, the prophets repeatedly described God as the true shepherd of his people. During Israel's exile and captivity, Ezekiel spoke of God as the good shepherd of the future, the one who would seek out the lost, rescue and heal them, and gather his people together (Ezekiel 34). This same prophet spoke of a future Messiah who would shepherd God's people like King David after the loss of Israel's monarchy.

Jesus is the true Shepherd, the One who knows, gathers, and protects the sheep. The most outstanding feature of this good shepherd, a unique characteristic that transcends even the images from the prophets, is that he "lays down his life for the sheep" (John 10:11). This total dedication and self-sacrifice of the good shepherd clearly distinguishes him from the hired man, who is motivated by personal gain and will abandon the flock in times of danger.

Through the shepherd's ultimate sacrifice for his sheep, the world outside Israel will be drawn into the fold so that there will be "one flock, one shepherd" (John 10:16). Jesus' power to lay down his life and "to take it up again" (10:18), in the mystery of his death and resurrection, reveals God's love for the world. Jesus' own sheep and his "other sheep" (10:16) outside the fold of Israel describe the full extent of God's saving will for all people and the universal scope of the Christian mission.

MEDITATIO

Reflect on these Scriptures from within your own searching, hurting, insecurity, and hope. Consider God's work within your own life and the salvation he is offering to you.

- The signs and wonders worked by Jesus and the apostles are quite different from magical deeds done to amaze people. Why was Peter able to work wonders in Jerusalem? In what ways are miracles tangible signs of salvation?

- Peter chose to heal the lame man who was begging for alms at the gate of the Temple. Why do you suppose he chose to heal this man and not others? Why did the author of Acts decide to include this particular healing in his account of the early Church?

- Luke makes it clear throughout Acts that Jesus was crucified because of the deeds of Jewish and Roman leaders, Jews and Gentiles, not only those involved in the historical decision to put Jesus to death, but also the human race throughout time. In what sense are you guilty of the death of Jesus and in need of repentance?

- The "one flock" and the "one shepherd" (John 10:16) refer to the whole Church united under Christ. This is the goal of the Christian mission and the ecumenical work of the Church. In what ways does the Church today continue this work of the Good Shepherd?

- Peter said that Jesus is the way to salvation for the whole human race. Jesus describes the full extent of the Church's universal mission by speaking of the one flock, uniting his own sheep and his other sheep outside the fold of Israel. What are the implications of this worldwide vision for the Church and for your role within it?

ORATIO

⋏

Offer to God what you have discovered in yourself from your meditation. Begin your prayer with these words, and then continue in your own words:

Good Shepherd, every day someone is placed in my path who is in need of healing and peace. Teach me to be aware of the healing power I possess through your Spirit. Help me not to be so busy that I fail to do the good that you are calling me to do. Motivate me to reach out to suffering people in your name.

When the words of prayer begin to seem inadequate and no longer necessary, move into the wordless prayer of contemplatio.

CONTEMPLATIO

⋏

Consider the image of Jesus, the Good Shepherd, in your imagination. Rest with this image, and believe that he is working with you—protecting, strengthening, healing, and empowering you.

OPERATIO

⋏

If we are to be disciples of Jesus, our lives and activities must express a healing dimension. What kinds of suffering and pain do you encounter most frequently in those around you? In what ways can you offer healing to them in the name of Jesus?

Fifth Sunday of Easter

LECTIO

⅄

Approach these texts with expectant faith, trusting that God wishes to transform your heart with the power of his word. When you are prepared, read these texts aloud, reading with your eyes and lips and listening with your ears and your heart. Hear these inspired words in a new way, guided by God's renewing Spirit.

ACTS 9:26-31

When Saul arrived in Jerusalem he tried to join the disciples, but they were all afraid of him, not believing that he was a disciple. Then Barnabas took charge of him and brought him to the apostles, and he reported to them how he had seen the Lord, and that he had spoken to him, and how in Damascus he had spoken out boldly in the name of Jesus. He moved about freely with them in Jerusalem, and spoke out boldly in the name of the Lord. He also spoke and debated with the Hellenists, but they tried to kill him. And when the brothers learned of this, they took him down to Caesarea and sent him on his way to Tarsus.

The church throughout all Judea, Galilee, and Samaria was at peace. It was being built up and walked in the fear of the Lord, and with the consolation of the Holy Spirit it grew in numbers.

∧

This scene is part of the narrative of Acts recounting Saul's transformation from the Church's most notorious enemy to its greatest evangelist. While Saul was on his way to Damascus, his life was radically changed when he encountered the risen Lord. In Damascus this persecutor of the Church "had spoken out boldly in the name of Jesus" (Acts 9:27). Clearly, he had been converted for a purpose, called to bear fruit for God's kingdom.

When Saul arrives in Jerusalem, Barnabas acts as his mediator with the leaders of the Church. It is critical that the new mission of Saul be rooted in the group of apostles who were with Jesus during his earthly ministry. They represent the tradition that began in Jesus, the Jerusalem community from which the worldwide Church would extend.

Both the intense personal encounter with Jesus that Saul experienced on the road and the apostolic tradition to which he was linked in Jerusalem were necessary for his authentic witness of Jesus. Saul's unique call from Christ and the call of the Church were two sides of the same vocation as evangelizer of the nations. Although Saul's early ministry was costly and surrounded by mistrust, his enthusiasm for the mission and fidelity to the call would continue to impel him from Jerusalem to the ends of the earth.

JOHN 15:1-8

Jesus said to his disciples: "I am the true vine, and my Father is the vine grower. He takes away every branch in me that does not bear fruit, and every one that does he prunes so that it bears more fruit. You are already pruned because of the word that I spoke to you. Remain in me, as I remain in you. Just as a branch cannot bear fruit on its own unless it remains on the vine, so neither can you unless you remain in me. I am the vine, you are the branches. Whoever remains in me and I in him will bear much fruit, because without me you can do nothing. Anyone who does not remain in me will be thrown out like a branch and wither; people will gather them and throw them into a fire and they will be burned. If you remain in me and my words remain in you, ask for whatever you want and it will be done for you. By this is my Father glorified, that you bear much fruit and become my disciples."

Grapevines covered the hillsides of Jesus' world, and the prophets called Israel the vineyard of God. Although God spaded, planted, and nourished the vineyard, he was rewarded with only wild and sour grapes. Isaiah proclaimed that in the days to come, Israel would take root, put forth shoots, blossom, and fill the whole world with fruit (27:6). Jesus announces that he is "the true vine" (John 15:1), fulfilling Israel's destiny and bringing forth fruit for all people.

We are the branches that make up the vine that is Jesus. We receive life from him not by being merely connected to him; we share in his life by becoming part of him. Jesus not only gives us life; he lives his life in us so that we are fully united with him and live in him. When we are united with Jesus in faith, we actually live with his life and love with his love. This mystical union between

Jesus and believers is expressed by Jesus' exhortation: "Remain in me, as I remain in you" (John 15:4).

The source of this union of life and love is the Father, "the vine grower" (John 15:1). He knows that he must do two things for ensuring maximum fruit production: he removes the branches that bear no fruit, and he prunes the branches that bear fruit so that they produce more fruit. Although some branches must be cut off in order to increase the well-being of the vine, it is only the Father who performs such judgment. Vines allowed to grow without pruning will produce smaller and smaller grapes as the vines gradually return to their wild state.

The purpose and goal of the vine is producing fruit. Bearing much fruit brings glory to the Father and provides evidence of discipleship. A fruitful life is sustained by union with Jesus. The 'fruit" borne by disciples includes all the manifestations of growth in Christ: love of others, humility, self-giving, faithfulness, and service to others. This is the fruit that will last.

MEDITATIO

The Scriptures challenge us to accept discipline and costly discipleship in order to bear fruit for Christ and his Church. Consider the ways in which, by taking these Scriptures to heart, your life could be transformed.

- Saul experienced forgiveness both from God and from the community he sought to destroy. How did receiving forgiveness empower him to minister both boldly and humbly?

- How have you experienced forgiveness for your past mistakes and harmful desires toward others? For what do you need to receive forgiveness in order to serve Christ and his Church with more courage and freedom?

- Luke tells us that "Barnabas" means "son of encouragement" (Acts 4:36), an apt description of his work of supporting new members in the early Church. Because of Barnabas' ministry of encouragement, Saul became a fruit-bearing branch within the true vine. What new members of your community need support and encouragement from today's "sons and daughters of encouragement"?

- The Father's pruning of the vine represents the trials and discipline required of those who unite their lives with the loving and total sacrifice of Jesus. What pruning is necessary for the Church to bear more fruit in the world? How have you experienced pruning in order to produce fruit?

- What dead wood in your life needs to be cut off in order for you to be a more responsive disciple of Jesus? What part of your life needs to be pruned in order to encourage new growth?

ORATIO

⋏

After allowing yourself to be challenged by these Scriptures, respond to God with the prayer that arises from within you. Begin with these words, and allow them to spark your own words of prayer:

> Risen Lord, you called Saul from his state of zealous certainty to a condition of helpless dependence. Give me your humility to trust in your way for my life so that I can respond to your guidance and direction. Keep me united to you as a branch of the vine so that I may bear the fruit of generous service.

Continue to pour out your heart until words fail and no longer seem necessary.

CONTEMPLATIO

⋏

As you move into silent contemplative prayer, choose a word, phrase, or image from the Scriptures to be your focus. Just rest in God's presence, recalling and repeating the word, phrase, or image when you get distracted. Trust in the interior renewal that God desires for you.

OPERATIO

⋏

The word of God can change us, shape us, and move us toward a transformed life, as it did for Saul. Consider the thoughts that arose in your meditatio and the inner renewal that occurred in your contemplatio. What newness, growth, or movement have you noticed within yourself as a result of your lectio divina today?

Sixth Sunday of Easter

LECTIO

From the earliest days of the Church, disciples of Jesus have gathered on the Lord's Day to experience, in word and sacrament, his self-offering and his risen life. Prepare yourself to read these sacred texts, which the Church has proclaimed through the centuries in its liturgical assembly, asking the Holy Spirit to help you listen and respond to the *sacra pagina*.

ACTS 10:25-26, 34-35, 44-48

When Peter entered, Cornelius met him and, falling at his feet, paid him homage. Peter, however, raised him up, saying, "Get up. I myself am also a human being."

Then Peter proceeded to speak and said, "In truth, I see that God shows no partiality. Rather, in every nation whoever fears him and acts uprightly is acceptable to him."

While Peter was still speaking these things, the Holy Spirit fell upon all who were listening to the word. The circumcised believers who had accompanied Peter were astounded that the gift of the Holy Spirit should have been poured out on the Gentiles also, for they could hear them speaking in tongues and glorifying God. Then Peter responded, "Can anyone withhold the water for baptizing these people, who have received the Holy Spirit even as we have?" He ordered them to be baptized in the name of Jesus Christ.

∧

The experiences that led Peter to the house of Cornelius prepared the Church for a broader understanding of itself that would open the gospel to people of all nations. The Church had already overcome previous divisions between rich and poor, slave and free, male and female. Now the final barrier, the most difficult, was about to be broken. The racial, cultural, and religious wall that divided Jews and Gentiles was the supreme test of the power of God's Spirit at work among the early Christians.

Cornelius was truly an outsider—a Gentile military officer stationed in Caesarea, the capital of the Roman forces that held Israel in subjugation. In Cornelius, God was breaking down the barriers that for so long had been assumed to be God's will. Peter was the insider—the leader of the community of Jewish disciples. Yet Peter was led to understand that "God shows no partiality" (Acts 10:34). God treats everyone on the same basis, and people from every nation have the same potential access to God. Those who treat God with reverence and people with justice are ready for the saving revelation of God through Jesus Christ.

Peter takes the first step in opening the Church to Gentiles by walking through the open door of Cornelius' house. And while Peter is still preaching the word of God, the Holy Spirit is given to Cornelius and the other Gentiles who are listening to Peter. Since the coming of God's promised Spirit is the sign of the new era, this event has rightly been called the Pentecost of the Gentile world.

Peter understands the significance of the moment, and he instructs that these Gentiles be baptized in the name of Jesus Christ. Peter is the instrument of God's epoch-making work, showing that the Gentiles, too, are chosen for salvation, baptism, and membership in Christ's Church. The gospel is now ready to go into the entire world.

John 15:9-17

Jesus said to his disciples: "As the Father loves me, so I also love you. Remain in my love. If you keep my commandments, you will remain in my love, just as I have kept my Father's commandments and remain in his love.

"I have told you this so that my joy may be in you and your joy might be complete. This is my commandment: love one another as I love you. No one has greater love than this, to lay down one's life for one's friends. You are my friends if you do what I command you. I no longer call you slaves, because a slave does not know what his master is doing. I have called you friends, because I have told you everything I have heard from my Father. It was not you who chose me, but I who chose you and appointed you to go and bear fruit that will remain, so that whatever you ask the Father in my name he may give you. This I command you: love one another."

Love is the divine energy that binds the Father with Jesus and Jesus with his followers. Jesus teaches his disciples that because the Father loves him and Jesus loves his disciples, their task is essentially this: "Remain in my love" (John 15:9). As Jesus responded to the Father's love with obedient, sacrificial love for others, so the disciples must respond to the love of Jesus with obedient, self-giving love for one another. All that Jesus asks of his followers can be summarized in one great commandment: "Love one another as I love you" (15:12).

This energy of divine love—the Father for Jesus, Jesus for his disciples, and the disciples for one another—demonstrates that the obedience demanded in the Christian life is not grudging compliance. The commandments of Jesus are not to be obeyed out of a sense of obligation or fear; rather, they are motivated by love and their purpose is joy. Jesus tells his disciples that he has given all of these teachings "so that my joy may be in you and your joy might be complete" (John 15:11). This complete joy is an experience of God's life, the kind of lasting joy that no sadness or hardship can take away.

Jesus calls his disciples "friends" to express the kind of loving relationship he desires with them. A master generally tells his slaves only what they need to know to do their job; "a slave does not know what his master is doing." But friendship means sharing knowledge and insight: "I have called you friends, because I have told you everything I have heard from my Father" (John 15:15). The relationship between slave and master is based on obligation and earned privileges, while the relationship of friends is rooted in free will and generosity. This unearned, undeserved gift of friendship with Jesus gives disciples the freedom and motivation they need "to go and bear fruit that will remain" (15:16).

MEDITATIO

Having listened to the inspired texts of Acts and John's Gospel, reflect on the boundless love of God. Consider what personal messages and challenges these texts are offering to you.

- When we observe other people, we mainly perceive our surface differences. But when we try to perceive their core, we recognize our oneness. How did Peter experience his unity with Cornelius? What experiences have taught you this truth?

- The Spirit of God is about the business of tearing down barriers that divide people. What walls of prejudice and bias prevent the gospel from being truly universal today?

- The Church is catholic and apostolic because it encompasses the whole world and is rooted in the tradition of the apostles. How do these readings express these marks of the Church? What direction is needed in the Church today so that it can become more fully the "one, holy, catholic, and apostolic" Church that we profess in the Creed?

- Remaining in the love of Jesus is not just a static feeling or a sentimental emotion. It means loving as Jesus loves, giving of ourselves for others, and even laying down our lives for our friends. What is different about this love than other expressions of love offered to us by the world? When have you seen this divine love manifested in your life?

- Jesus said, "I no longer call you slaves. . . . I have called you friends" (John 15:15). Why do people sometimes feel like a slave of Jesus rather than his friend? What are the main differences? How can you better receive the friendship that Jesus offers you?

ORATIO

In response to the words of Peter and of Jesus, offer your prayer to God. Express the desires, hopes, and gratitude that fill your heart:

Savior of all nations, I can sometimes become very comfortable in my own culture, my own neighborhood, and my own biases. Yet you call your disciples to remove barriers and open doors that separate people from one another. Lead me to see other people as you see them and to offer them the love that you have for them.

Continue praying in your own words, using some of the words, thoughts, and images of the Scriptures.

CONTEMPLATIO

Consider that God looks upon all people with unconditional positive regard and unimaginable love. Spend a few moments in wordless prayer, seeking to receive a share of God's own universal love. Be still and feel your heart changing.

OPERATIO

As a disciple of Jesus, you are called to participate in the outward mission of the Church. Who are the outsiders in your community? What can you do to support the missionary activity of the Church and invite them into the community of faith?

The Ascension of the Lord

LECTIO

The risen Jesus tells his disciples to wait for the coming of the Holy Spirit. This feast of the Ascension urges us to wait expectantly for the movement and guidance of God's Spirit as we read these sacred texts.

Prepare yourself to listen to the Scriptures and to incorporate the meaning of the Ascension into your own discipleship. Ask the Holy Spirit to help you listen, reflect, and respond.

ACTS 1:1-11

In the first book, Theophilus, I dealt with all that Jesus did and taught until the day he was taken up, after giving instructions through the Holy Spirit to the apostles whom he had chosen. He presented himself alive to them by many proofs after he had suffered, appearing to them during forty days and speaking about the kingdom of God. While meeting with them, he enjoined them not to depart from Jerusalem, but to wait for "the promise of the Father about which you have heard me speak; for John baptized with water, but in a few days you will be baptized with the Holy Spirit."

When they had gathered together they asked him, "Lord, are you at this time going to restore the kingdom to Israel?" He answered them, "It is not for you to know the times or seasons that the Father has established by his own authority.

But you will receive power when the Holy Spirit comes upon you, and you will be my witnesses in Jerusalem, throughout Judea and Samaria, and to the ends of the earth." When he had said this, as they were looking on, he was lifted up, and a cloud took him from their sight. While they were looking intently at the sky as he was going, suddenly two men dressed in white garments stood beside them. They said, "Men of Galilee, why are you standing there looking at the sky? This Jesus who has been taken up from you into heaven will return in the same way as you have seen him going into heaven."

⋏

The narratives of the four Gospels do not speak of a time sequence separating the glorification of Jesus into distinct moments of resurrection, ascension, and the gift of the Spirit. Rather, at the end of each Gospel, the risen Jesus commissions his disciples to go forth and continue his work as he departs from them. But since human reality is bound by time and space, Luke narrates these mysteries as separate episodes in the Acts of the Apostles. Luke's descriptions of forty days and fifty days allow us to reflect on how the paschal mystery unfolds gradually for us, allowing us to be transformed step by step. So throughout the Easter season, we focus our attention, first, on one aspect of the mystery and, then, on another. On Easter we concentrate on Jesus' victory over sin and death; at the Ascension we contemplate his exaltation and enthronement with the Father. On Pentecost we will reflect on the gift of the Spirit.

The Book of Acts resumes the gospel story at the point where Jesus is "taken up" (1:2). Like Elijah, who was taken up to heaven in a whirlwind by a fiery chariot, and Moses, who according to Jewish tradition was taken up in a cloud at the end of his earthly life, so Jesus' earthly sojourn ends in the manner of these great figures. The missions of Elijah and Moses, however, were not finished at the end of their earthly lives; their successors carried on their work to its completion. Moses appointed Joshua to lead his people into the Promised Land, and Elijah placed his prophetic mantle over the shoulders of Elisha before he ascended. Likewise, Jesus entrusts his work to his disciples as he commissions them as his witnesses to the world.

The Evangelist Luke's two-volume work, his Gospel and Acts, divides salvation history into the period of Israel, the period of Jesus, and the period of the Spirit-directed Church. With the Ascension the time of Jesus ends, and the stage is set for the Spirit-led mission to begin on Pentecost. The apostles are the connecting link between the times of Jesus and of the Spirit. They have witnessed the life, death, and resurrection of Jesus, and after the Ascension they are sent out to bear witness to Jesus "to the ends of the earth" (Acts 1:8). This commission from the departing Jesus provides the mandate for the Church's missionary activity throughout the centuries.

MARK 16:15-20

Jesus said to his disciples: "Go into the whole world and proclaim the gospel to every creature. Whoever believes and is baptized will be saved; whoever does not believe will be condemned. These signs will accompany those who believe: in my name they will drive out demons, they will speak new languages. They will pick up serpents with their hands, and if they drink any deadly thing, it will not harm them. They will lay hands on the sick, and they will recover."

So then the Lord Jesus, after he spoke to them, was taken up into heaven and took his seat at the right hand of God. But they went forth and preached everywhere, while the Lord worked with them and confirmed the word through accompanying signs.

⋏

These final verses were added to Mark's Gospel in order to connect the narratives of the disciples throughout the Gospel with the ongoing history of the Church. These traditions, drawn from other New Testament writings, include Jesus' commission to proclaim the good news to the world, the call to faith and baptism, the tangible signs that will accompany belief, the ascension of Jesus to God's right hand, and the beginning of the disciples' mission.

After Jesus is "taken up into heaven" (Mark 16:19), he is no longer isolated by time and space as he was when he walked the roads of Palestine. The fact that he is no longer among us in his flesh allows us to know him widely—he dwells in us interiorly, and we know him through the life and sacraments of the Church. As Lord of heaven and earth, Jesus holds all things in his loving care, and all people are called to share in the divine life he offers.

The "accompanying signs" (Mark 16:20) specified in the Gospel were powerful signs in the ancient world. They may not be the same signs that accompany Christian faith today, but the signs we witness are just as powerful. Through the power of the risen Lord, people give up their crippling addictions and reunite with their forgiving families. The memories of those damaged by a painful childhood are healed, and victims look toward a happy future. The darkness of depression is lifted as people lift their faces and see the light. Those tortured by a life of sin are freed from their demons through the power of love. In all of these ways, the Lord confirms the word through accompanying signs. Signs like these happen every day. As disciples of Jesus, we must testify to them, affirm the power of faith, and with expectant faith believe that the Lord will continue to work in the world today.

MEDITATIO

Reflect on the glorification and exaltation of Jesus as the Scriptures unfold the paschal mystery. Explore the ways that God's word challenges you to be transformed, step by step.

- The risen Jesus tells his disciples to wait for the coming of the Holy Spirit. This feast of the Ascension urges us also to wait with hope and confidence, although waiting is not something that we naturally like to do. Why, in God's plan, is it often necessary for us to wait? What have you learned through the practice of waiting?

- When the disciples ask to know God's timetable, Jesus responds, "It is not for you to know the times or seasons that the Father has established by his own authority" (Acts 1:7). How do Christians guard against uninformed speculation about Christ's future coming and still maintain a lively apocalyptic hope?

- The two men in white garments ask the disciples, "Why are you standing there looking at the sky?" (Acts 1:11). We have work to do, a mission to fulfill. How are you called by Jesus to be his witness in the world?

- The ascension of Jesus joins his glorified humanity with the mission of the Church. Jesus "took his seat at the right hand of God," and the disciples "went forth and preached everywhere" (Mark 16:19, 20). In what ways does the work of the Church confirm both the absence and the presence of its glorified Lord?

- The risen Lord assures his disciples that signs will confirm the word and accompany those who believe. What signs have you witnessed that confirm the good news of the gospel and accompany the faith of believers?

ORATIO

After listening and meditating on these Scriptures, respond to God's word through the words of your prayer:

Lord Jesus, you are risen and alive, and you empower me to be your witness in the world. Open my eyes to see the signs of your presence around me, and open my mouth to speak the good news. Give me confidence that you work within me through the power of your Spirit.

Continue praying in your own words, using the words and images of the Scriptures that you have made your own.

CONTEMPLATIO

Sit in quiet waiting, trusting that the Spirit of God fills your heart. Let the Holy Spirit enkindle your heart with the fire of divine love and transform your life from the inside out.

OPERATIO

The feast of the Ascension challenges us to wait for the coming of the Holy Spirit at Pentecost. Yet the apostles show us that waiting is not about sitting on your hands, but lifting them in confident and hopeful prayer. How does Jesus want you to wait for the Holy Spirit during the coming days?

Seventh Sunday of Easter

LECTIO

⋏

This final Sunday before Pentecost invites us to reflect on the early Church and on our own call to be witnesses to the resurrection by the newness of our lives. Call upon the renewing Spirit of God as you prepare to read the inspired Scriptures. Open yourself to whatever new insight or encouragement God wishes to offer you.

Acts 1:15-17, 20A, 20C-26

Peter stood up in the midst of the brothers—there was a group of about one hundred and twenty persons in the one place—. He said, "My brothers, the Scripture had to be fulfilled which the Holy Spirit spoke beforehand through the mouth of David, concerning Judas, who was the guide for those who arrested Jesus. He was numbered among us and was allotted a share in this ministry.

"For it is written in the Book of Psalms: *May another take his office.*

"Therefore, it is necessary that one of the men who accompanied us the whole time the Lord Jesus came and went among us, beginning from the baptism of John until the day on which he was taken up from us, become with us a witness to his resurrection." So they proposed two, Judas called Barsabbas, who was also known as Justus, and

Matthias. Then they prayed, "You, Lord, who know the hearts of all, show which one of these two you have chosen to take the place in this apostolic ministry from which Judas turned away to go to his own place." Then they gave lots to them, and the lot fell upon Matthias, and he was counted with the eleven apostles.

∧

As the apostles waited in Jerusalem for the coming of the Holy Spirit, they discerned through prayer and Scripture that they should choose another apostle to fill the spot left by Judas after his betrayal and suicide. Someone must take his office of responsibility within the core circle of apostles, as there must again be twelve apostles before the Spirit descends to empower the apostolic Church.

Peter addresses the community about the process for replacing Judas. He states that the candidate must be "one of the men who accompanied us the whole time the Lord Jesus came and went among us" (Acts 1:21). This span of witness includes the entire time of Jesus' ministry and teaching, from the baptizing of John to the ascension of Jesus. The unique qualifications of this office demonstrate its foundational role for the Church.

Two men are put forward for the apostolic ministry: Barsabbas and Matthias. The final choice, however, is left to God, accompanied by the prayer of the community. Through the casting of lots, the Lord's choice of Matthias is made clear. The decision is made both on qualifications and on divine choice. It is made from below, from the ranks of those whom the prayerful community chooses, and from above, as God graciously guides his Church to fulfill its mission.

Matthias is then counted with the eleven apostles, and the number is restored to twelve. The twelve apostles link the Church to the events that originated the Church, and through their "witness to his resurrection" (Acts 1:22), they lead the Church to fulfill its mission. With Peter, they testify to what has happened so that it may continue to happen within the Church. With the twelve apostles restored, the community is ready for the coming of the Holy Spirit.

JOHN 17:11B-19

Lifting up his eyes to heaven, Jesus prayed, saying: "Holy Father, keep them in your name that you have given me, so that they may be one just as we are one. When I was with them I protected them in your name that you gave me, and I guarded them, and none of them was lost except the son of destruction, in order that the Scripture might be fulfilled. But now I am coming to you. I speak this in the world so that they may share my joy completely. I gave them your word, and the world hated them, because they do not belong to the world any more than I belong to the world. I do not ask that you take them out of the world but that you keep them from the evil one. They do not belong to the world any more than I belong to the world. Consecrate them in the truth. Your word is truth. As you sent me into the world, so I sent them into the world. And I consecrate myself for them, so that they also may be consecrated in truth."

$$\Lambda$$

In Jesus' parting prayer to the Father, he gives voice to his deepest hopes for his disciples. His own mission in the world is coming to an end, but that of the disciples is about to begin. Jesus prays that the disciples may experience the unity he shares with his Father, that they may share in his joy, that they may be protected from the evil one, and that they may be consecrated in truth.

As Jesus leaves his disciples, he knows they will be persecuted by the world, just as he was. Yet Jesus does not ask the Father to take them out of the world, but rather to protect them from the world's evil powers. The disciples of Jesus no more belong to the world than he himself does, yet Jesus knows that they will be physically present there even when he is not. On the one hand, Jesus does not want them to withdraw from the world into an otherworldly enclave, but on the other hand, he does not want them to become indistinguishable from the world.

In order to prepare for and succeed in their mission in the world, the disciples must be holy as God is holy. So Jesus prays that the Father will "consecrate," or make holy, his disciples "in the truth" (John 17:17). In addition to the work of the Father, this consecration in the truth involves the work of both the Son and the Holy Spirit. Unity with Jesus, who is the way, the truth, and the life, will equip the disciples for service in his name. Jesus consecrates himself for them through his total self-gift on the cross. As the disciples share in this total gift of love, they are made holy in the truth. Unity with the Holy Spirit, who is the Spirit of truth, will consecrate believers in the truth so that they can know, love, and serve their holy God.

MEDITATIO

∧

Having listened to the inspired texts of Acts and John's Gospel, let these Scriptures interact with your own prayerful waiting for the Spirit. Consider what personal messages and challenges these texts are offering to you.

- The process for replacing Judas among the twelve apostles forms a precedent for how to make decisions as a community, looking to God to show the way. What elements of this process of discernment can help the Church make decisions today?

- Peter describes the passage that he quotes from the Book of Psalms as a revelation from God, that is, Scripture "which the Holy Spirit spoke . . . through the mouth of David" (Acts 1:16). In what ways does this description of Scripture imply both its divine and human origins?

- Peter's speech about Judas is a sober reminder that traitors can and will enter the ranks of the Church's leaders. In fact, Peter himself fled in the darkness and stridently denied his Lord. What do the sagas of Peter and Judas tell you about the nature of the Church and its leadership? About ourselves as frail human beings?

- Jesus says of his disciples, "They do not belong to the world any more than I belong to the world" (John 17:16).

What are the challenges of living in the world but not belonging to the world?

• What is the role of the Father, the Son, and the Holy Spirit in the consecration of Jesus' disciples? How do you experience the work of the Trinity in your own desire for holiness?

ORATIO

After listening to God's word in the Scriptures, respond to God's word through the prayer that rises from your heart:

Holy Father, you sent your Son into the world, and he has sent me into the world, although neither of us belongs to the world. Make me holy so that I may bear witness to the name of Jesus through what I say and do. Send me your Spirit to dwell in my heart and guide my life in the truth.

Continue praying in your own words, modeling your prayer on the prayer of Jesus.

CONTEMPLATIO

When words are no longer necessary in your prayer, offer silent praise to the Father, Son, and Holy Spirit. Realize that you share in the unity, joy, love, and holiness of God.

OPERATIO

You have been chosen by Jesus to be a witness to his resurrection. Consider how you can manifest the resurrection to others through the holiness of your life in union with God. Change one aspect of your life to make it new in Christ as you await the Spirit of Pentecost.

Pentecost Sunday

LECTIO

As you prepare to hear the Scriptures for the feast of Pentecost, become aware of the rhythm of your breathing. Breathe in, being filled with the presence of God's Spirit. Breathe out, letting go of your preoccupations and anxieties.

Listen for God's word to you within these sacred texts. Let God's renewing Spirit guide you to hear these Scriptures in a new way.

ACTS 2:1-11

When the time for Pentecost was fulfilled, they were all in one place together. And suddenly there came from the sky a noise like a strong driving wind, and it filled the entire house in which they were. Then there appeared to them tongues as of fire, which parted and came to rest on each one of them. And they were all filled with the Holy Spirit and began to speak in different tongues, as the Spirit enabled them to proclaim.

Now there were devout Jews from every nation under heaven staying in Jerusalem. At this sound, they gathered in a large crowd, but they were confused because each one heard them speaking in his own language. They were astounded, and in amazement they asked, "Are not all these people who are speaking Galileans? Then how does each of us hear them in his native language? We are Parthians, Medes, and Elamites, inhabitants of Mesopotamia, Judea and Cappadocia,

Pontus and Asia, Phrygia and Pamphylia, Egypt and the districts of Libya near Cyrene, as well as travelers from Rome, both Jews and converts to Judaism, Cretans and Arabs, yet we hear them speaking in our own tongues of the mighty acts of God."

⌒

Fifty days after Easter, as the disciples of Jesus are gathered for prayer in Jerusalem, the Holy Spirit comes upon them in dramatic fashion. With the sound of a driving wind and flames of fire resting on each person, the Spirit sets in motion preaching, prophecy, conversion, and a worldwide mission. The disciples begin to speak in different languages, and wondrously their proclamation of the good news of Jesus is heard and understood by Jewish pilgrims from distant and exotic lands with many different native languages.

It is uncertain whether the disciples from Galilee spoke their own native Aramaic and were understood by all the foreigners or whether they spoke in all those different languages. In either case, the point is that the miracle of the first Pentecost reverses the story of the Tower of Babel. In that account from Genesis, God confused the languages of humankind in response to human arrogance, and they were scattered over the face of the earth. Now the good news of Jesus Christ is the language that unites all these different peoples.

Pentecost is the first phase of the dramatic story of the Church as told in the Acts of the Apostles. The rest of Acts narrates the spread of the gospel and the growth of the Church, moving from Jerusalem through Samaria, Syria, Asia Minor, Greece, and all the way to Rome. It moves first among Jews and then fans out to

Gentiles. With Paul's arrival in Rome at the end of Acts, the gospel has reached the heart of the Roman Empire and begins to transform the face of the earth.

Now, two millennia later, the Church's missionary activity continues on a global scale. Pentecost continues to challenge the Church to communicate the gospel in ever more effective ways to peoples in every land on earth. Like the early disciples who moved beyond the land of Israel and the Jewish people, we must help all the peoples of the world to hear and express the good news of Jesus in their own languages and within the context of their own cultures. For that ongoing mission, the Church always needs the transforming power and guidance of the Holy Spirit.

JOHN 15:26-27; 16:12-15[*]

Jesus said to his disciples: "When the Advocate comes whom I will send you from the Father, the Spirit of truth that proceeds from the Father, he will testify to me. And you also testify, because you have been with me from the beginning.

"I have much more to tell you, but you cannot bear it now. But when he comes, the Spirit of truth, he will guide you to all truth. He will not speak on his own, but he will speak what he hears, and will declare to you the things that are coming. He will glorify me, because he will take from what is mine and declare it to you. Everything that the Father has is mine; for this reason I told you that he will take from what is mine and declare it to you."

ᐱ

---

[*] John 20:19-23, used for Pentecost Sunday, Year A, is also an option for Year B.

The Advocate, or Spirit of truth, that the glorified Jesus sends from the Father is the Holy Spirit, the enlightening, renewing, transforming Spirit of God who dwells with the Church. Jesus is more present and alive with his people today in the Spirit than he ever was to his disciples during his earthly life. In those days, Jesus lived *with* his disciples; after he is glorified, Jesus lives *in* his disciples through the Spirit.

The Spirit of truth will guide believers "to all truth" (John 16:13). If our understanding of Jesus were limited to only what Jesus was able to convey to his followers during his public life on earth, our belief would be as inadequate as that of the disciples before the resurrection. But the Holy Spirit enlightens disciples to understand and experience the truth of Christ much more richly. Because of the Spirit, Jesus is not a distant figure from the past; he is the living Lord of our lives. Through the Spirit of truth, the whole mystery of Jesus—his words, actions, death, and resurrection—can be understood, internalized, and lived in a much more complete way.

The gift of the Spirit signals a new stage in the history of salvation: the age of the Church. Between the resurrection of Jesus and his final coming in glory, the community of disciples experiences Jesus Christ in the sacramental worship and Spirit-guided teaching of the Church. The Holy Spirit testifies to Jesus, guiding the Church "to all truth" and declaring to the Church "the things that are coming" (John 16:13). Through the work of the Spirit in the ongoing life of the Church, the "much more" (16:12) that Jesus wished to tell his disciples during his ministry will be gradually revealed.

MEDITATIO

⋏

Reflect on these Scriptures of Pentecost in the midst of your own desires and hopes. Consider God's promises to you and how God wishes to dwell with you.

- Red is the liturgical color for Pentecost, and many parishes invite all those who gather for Mass to wear red on that day. Red recalls the flames of the Holy Spirit and also reminds us of the sacrifice and martyrdom awaiting Jesus' disciples. In what ways does the color red express the emotions that fill your heart at the conclusion of this season of Easter?

- The Church must effectively communicate the gospel for peoples of different languages and cultures throughout the world. What are some of the challenges and dangers in translating the message of Jesus into other languages and cultural contexts? How can you best translate the message of Jesus to a secular culture?

- The Holy Spirit blows through the Church, searching for hearts willing to be transformed by grace. What fire of grace do you wish to be lit in your heart?

- Jesus said, "I have much more to tell you, but you cannot bear it now. But when he comes, the Spirit of truth, he will guide you to all truth" (John 16:12-13). Why was Jesus unable to say to his disciples many of the things he had to tell them? In what way does the Holy Spirit, present in the community of disciples, guide the Church to all truth?

- In what way can it be said that Jesus is more present to his disciples today than he was with his disciples during his earthly ministry? What are the results of this intimacy with Jesus in your own life?

ORATIO

Call upon God's Spirit to bless you in response to the needs you have discovered within yourself through your meditatio. Begin your prayer with these words, and then continue in your own words:

Come, Holy Spirit, empower your Church to transform the world with your truth. Guide me into the fullness of truth, and help me comprehend the mystery of Christ in all its richness and depth.

When the words of prayer begin to seem inadequate and no longer necessary, move into the wordless prayer of contemplatio.

CONTEMPLATIO

The glorified Christ dwells with you and within you through the presence of the Holy Spirit. Pray that God's Spirit transform you from within, making you a person of hope so that you can entrust your future to God.

OPERATIO

人

The seven gifts of the Holy Spirit, derived from Isaiah 11:2-3, are given in the Sacrament of Baptism and strengthened in the Sacrament of Confirmation. These are wisdom; understanding; counsel (right judgment); fortitude (courage); knowledge; piety (reverence); and fear of the Lord (wonder and awe). Choose one of these gifts, and ask the Holy Spirit to more fully activate that gift within you this Pentecost.

Chapter Five

Lectio Divina for the Easter Season: Year C

Easter Sunday of the Resurrection of the Lord

LECTIO

∧

Kiss the biblical text, or place your palms upon it as an expression of your reverence toward God's word. Ask the Holy Spirit to lead you through this lectio divina, to guide your understanding, and to enkindle within you the fire of divine love.

Begin reading when you feel ready to hear God's voice speaking through Scripture. Slowly articulate the words so that you can listen better as you read.

ACTS 10:34A, 37-43

Peter proceeded to speak and said: "You know what has happened all over Judea, beginning in Galilee after the baptism that John preached, how God anointed Jesus of Nazareth with the Holy Spirit and power. He went about doing good and healing all those oppressed by the devil, for God was with him. We are witnesses of all that he did both in the country of the Jews and in Jerusalem. They put him to death by hanging him on a tree. This man God raised on the third day and granted that he be visible, not to all the people, but to us, the witnesses chosen by God in advance, who ate and drank with him after he rose from the dead. He commissioned us to preach to the people and testify that he is the one appointed by God as judge of the living and the dead. To him all the prophets bear witness, that everyone who believes in him will receive forgiveness of sins through his name."

∧

What a transformation has been made in Peter, from his cowardice at Jesus' passion to the testimony he courageously offers here to the Gentile household of Cornelius. Once the frightened denier, he is now the bold testifier to everything that God is doing in Jesus. Through his shameful experience and Jesus' forgiveness, Peter has learned that the most important work of a disciple is to publicly profess, in word and in deed, that Jesus Christ is Lord.

Peter's address is a concise, densely packed account of all that Jesus has done and meant for his followers. Three times Peter uses the word "witness" (Acts 10: 39, 41, 43). First, he describes himself and the other apostles as witnesses of all that Jesus did throughout his earthly ministry on earth. Then, Peter describes himself and the apostles as witnesses chosen by God to experience his risen life. Those who have seen the Lord, "who ate and drank with him after he rose from the dead" (10:41), share a commission to testify to Christ's exaltation. And finally, Peter says that all the prophets of old bear witness to Jesus and to the divine forgiveness he offers.

Ancient Scripture and new testimony from the apostles give witness to Jesus. They testify to the salvation he offers to those who believe in him and accept the new life he offers them through the resurrection. Those to whom Peter speaks do not have the advantage of witnessing the earthly life of Jesus or seeing his resurrection appearances. Nor do we, yet we receive the same invitation to faith. So at Easter, we listen to Peter's witness, accept the healing and forgiveness offered to us by Jesus, and join with the apostles and prophets as witnesses of the risen Lord.

After listening to the testimony of Peter, begin reading the Gospel when you are ready. Read this familiar account as if for the first time. Listen with expectation, confident that God will teach you something new through the words of the Gospel according to Luke.

LUKE 24:1-12*

At daybreak on the first day of the week the women who had come from Galilee with Jesus took the spices they had prepared and went to the tomb. They found the stone rolled away from the tomb; but when they entered, they did not find the body of the Lord Jesus. While they were puzzling over this, behold, two men in dazzling garments appeared to them. They were terrified and bowed their faces to the ground. They said to them, "Why do you seek the living one among the dead? He is not here, but he has been raised. Remember what he said to you while he was still in Galilee, that the Son of Man must be handed over to sinners and be crucified, and rise on the third day." And they remembered his words. Then they returned from the tomb and announced all these things to the eleven and to all the others. The women were Mary Magdalene, Joanna, and Mary the mother of James; the others who accompanied them also told this to the apostles, but their story seemed like nonsense and they did not believe them. But Peter got up and ran to

---

*This is the reading for the Easter Vigil Mass and an alternative reading for Easter Day. The reading for Easter Day is John 20:1-9.

the tomb, bent down, and saw the burial cloths alone; then he went home amazed at what had happened.

Although the empty tomb might hint at a reversal of the tragedy of Jesus' death when read in the light of Easter faith, it only leaves the women perplexed. Then the sight of two heavenly messengers terrifies the women, and they bow to the ground. At the door of the tomb, the realm of death, the women hear an affirmation of life, and they challenge the women's focus on the tomb: "Why do you seek the living one among the dead? He is not here, but he has been raised" (Luke 24:5-6).

The messengers summon the women to remember Jesus' words—that as the suffering Son of Man, Jesus would be handed over to crucifixion, and then he would rise on the third day. Joyously remembering these words, the women announce all these things to "the eleven" apostles (Luke 24:9) and the other disciples. Only after remembering these words do the women become heralds of the resurrection. The enduring power of Jesus' words reverberates through the Lukan resurrection appearances, just as the power of the risen Jesus himself will do as he breaks open the Scriptures for his followers.

The women's story seems like an absurd attempt to challenge reality. No one believes them, except perhaps Peter. His denials have instilled in him a greater trust. He runs to the tomb, peers into it, and sees only the linen cloths without the body of Jesus, just as the women have said. The cloths suggest that Jesus has previously been in the tomb but is there no longer. If the body of Jesus has been stolen, surely the cloths would not still be there. Peter is left in amazement.

Luke invites his readers, along with the disciples, to ponder this mystery. Perplexity, disbelief, and amazement mix with hints of something more wondrous than anyone can imagine. What can explain these events? Could Jesus be alive after all? Do we dare to hope in the resurrection? What seems to have been an end has now become a new beginning.

MEDITATIO

Spend some time reflecting on these two Scriptures, which recall the experiences of Easter by the first Christians. Consider your own Easter experiences, and seek the meaning of these texts for your own discipleship.

- Christians today experience the resurrection in the ways they see Christ's living presence in the world. In what ways is your perception of the resurrection different from that of the women at the tomb? In what ways are they similar?

- Peter speaks of three ways that the apostles and prophets witness to Jesus. In what ways are people today called to be witnesses of Jesus' resurrection?

- Both the Gospel and the Acts of Luke highlight the experience of Peter. How has Jesus prepared Peter to be a witness to his resurrection? How does Peter serve as an example to you?

- Luke's first resurrection narrative describes the response of the women and Peter, and it ends in open-ended amazement. In what sense does Luke present the events at the empty tomb as a moment of reflection, decision, and faith for his readers?

- As Christians, we are Easter people. We do not merely put on new clothes for Easter, but we put on new lives. How are you experiencing transformation as you listen to and reflect on these Scriptures?

ORATIO

Respond in faith to the message of resurrection and life you have heard in these Scriptures. Begin to pray in these words:

Risen Lord, fill me with astonishment and awe at the mystery of your resurrection. May your heavenly messengers lead me to discover the wonderful news and the transforming power of your resurrection.

Continue praying from your heart in the words God's Spirit gives you.

CONTEMPLATIO

⅄

Through Christ, life has conquered death, and we now experience the inauguration of a new creation and a new way of looking at life. As you contemplate Christ's resurrection and the new life he has given you, allow yourself to be transformed from the inside out.

OPERATIO

⅄

The angels' message of resurrection is that Christ is not "here" (Luke 24:6), inhabiting the realm of the dead, but has emptied death of its power. Christians today are summoned to live, proclaim, and celebrate this victory by resisting all those forms of death and violence that saturate our culture. How can you witness to the resurrection this week?

Second Sunday of Easter

LECTIO

⋀

Close off the day's distractions, and enter a quiet time for these moments with God's inspired word. Become aware of your breath as a gift of God, breathing in as you are filled with the presence of God, breathing out as you let go of all unnecessary anxiety.

Begin reading when you feel ready to hear God's voice in the sacred text.

ACTS 5:12-16

Many signs and wonders were done among the people at the hands of the apostles. They were all together in Solomon's portico. None of the others dared to join them, but the people esteemed them. Yet more than ever, believers in the Lord, great numbers of men and women, were added to them. Thus they even carried the sick out into the streets and laid them on cots and mats so that when Peter came by, at least his shadow might fall on one or another of them. A large number of people from the towns in the vicinity of Jerusalem also gathered, bringing the sick and those disturbed by unclean spirits, and they were all cured.

⋀

The reason Christianity began and has flourished for two thousand years is because of the resurrection of Jesus. The early

Christians knew that through Jesus, they had been freed from the domination of sin and death to experience a new and eternal life. The resurrection explains why the early Church succeeded, and the success of the early Church is proof of the power of Jesus' resurrection.

Acts points to the parallels between the ministry of Jesus and the ministry of the apostles. Just as the earthly Jesus brought physical and spiritual healing to people, so the apostles performed "signs and wonders" (Acts 5:12) on behalf of the sick and the possessed. The early Church extended compassion and welcome to the sick in a culture that often linked sin with suffering and that regarded sick persons as being under the power of evil spirits. It did so in confidence that Jesus' death and resurrection had broken the power of the evil one, that there was nothing to fear from contact with outcasts, and that the sick and suffering were God's beloved ones. The ministry of the apostles was viewed with high esteem by the people, and many men and women were added to the believing community.

Peter had followed Jesus from town to town, watching him cure the sick and heal the hopeless from despair. Now the crowds were following Peter around the streets of Jerusalem, bringing their sick on cots and mats, hoping his shadow would fall over them with a blessing. This detail demonstrates the extent of Christ's power working through him. It was not necessarily the direct touch or even awareness of Peter that brought healing to people's lives. Rather, their cures occurred through faith in Jesus that the presence of Peter inspired in them. Peter had become so transformed through God's Spirit working within him that his closeness conveyed something of the presence of Jesus to people.

The world still looks to believers in Jesus to inspire and mediate his healing presence. Today's disciples must bring the light of the risen Lord and the truth of reconciliation with God wherever we go. We have been commissioned by Jesus to carry his Holy Spirit with us as we come in contact with people each day. We are the living signs that evil has been defeated, that death has been overcome by life, and that sin has been overpowered by divine mercy. The crowds are still looking for signs and wonders. They must be able to look to us, to the Church of Jesus Christ, as we allow faith in the resurrection of Jesus to guide us through the streets of our world.

JOHN 20:19-31

On the evening of that first day of the week, when the doors were locked, where the disciples were, for fear of the Jews, Jesus came and stood in their midst and said to them, "Peace be with you." When he had said this, he showed them his hands and his side. The disciples rejoiced when they saw the Lord. Jesus said to them again, "Peace be with you. As the Father has sent me, so I send you." And when he had said this, he breathed on them and said to them, "Receive the Holy Spirit. Whose sins you forgive are forgiven them, and whose sins you retain are retained."

Thomas, called Didymus, one of the Twelve, was not with them when Jesus came. So the other disciples said to him, "We have seen the Lord." But he said to them, "Unless I see the mark of the nails in his hands and put my finger into the nailmarks and put my hand into his side, I will not believe."

Now a week later his disciples were again inside and Thomas was with them. Jesus came, although the doors were locked, and stood in their midst and said, "Peace be with you." Then he said to Thomas, "Put your finger here and see my hands, and bring your hand and put it into my side, and do not be unbelieving, but believe." Thomas answered and said to him, "My Lord and my God!" Jesus said to him, "Have you come to believe because you have seen me? Blessed are those who have not seen and have believed."

Now Jesus did many other signs in the presence of his disciples that are not written in this book. But these are written that you may come to believe that Jesus is the Christ, the Son of God, and that through this belief you may have life in his name.

What Jesus had promised his disciples—peace, joy, and the Holy Spirit—they now receive through their encounter with the risen Lord. Jesus equips the disciples with everything they need to continue his mission. Then, having received these gifts, Jesus sends the disciples on mission to share those gifts with others in the world.

Opening the locked doors of their hearts to recognize that he is standing in their midst, Jesus offers his disciples the familiar greeting that will forever have a new and deep meaning for them: "Peace be with you" (John 20:19). Jesus offers them a peace that is not just a passive absence of conflict; it has been won at the price of his cross and resurrection. As if to remind his disciples of this gift of peace, he immediately shows them his wounded hands and side. The disciples respond to his words and wounds by rejoicing, expressing the gift of joy that the sorrows of the world cannot steal.

Then Jesus tells them that his gift of peace is also a call to mission—the continuation of the mission on which his Father had sent him and for which they will need the life of his Spirit.

Jesus breathes on his disciples with his divine Spirit, the breath that God had breathed into the nostrils of human dust at creation. The breath of Jesus creates the disciples anew from the dust of fear and despair. On that Easter Day of new creation, they are sent on the mission of reconciling sinners to the Father. They are sent as living witnesses that the pain of violent wounds can be healed and that the hatred that inflicts piercing hurts can be transformed into joy and peace through the power of the Holy Spirit. They must not remain huddled behind locked doors; instead, they are sent by the risen Christ to continue his mission of healing and forgiving.

MEDITATIO

Allow the book of Scripture and the book of your life to "dialogue" so that you come to understand the significance of these texts for you during this Easter season.

- Without the resurrection of Jesus, our faith is empty and our proclamation is in vain. Why is the resurrection the foundational event of the Church and the reason the Church has prospered for two millennia?

- The people of Jerusalem brought the sick out into the streets so that at least the shadow of Peter would fall on them. What does this tell you about the character and influence of Peter in the early Christian community?

- People still look for signs and wonders today. What do people see in your life that helps them to believe?

- How do Jesus' gifts of peace, joy, and the Holy Spirit equip the Church for its mission in the world? How might greater attention to these gifts of the risen Lord help the Church be a clearer sign of Christ's reconciling presence?

- The risen Jesus said, "Blessed are those who have not seen and have believed" (John 20:29). He was addressing the first readers of John's Gospel and all of us who have not seen the empty tomb or the risen Jesus. How does your listening to God's word in Scripture help you to believe?

ORATIO

Prayer begins by listening to God's word with a receptive mind, followed by meditation on that word until the truth of that word leads to real understanding. When you are ready to respond to God's word with the words of your own prayer, you might begin like this:

My Lord and my God, you have brought new life to the world through the resurrection, and you have renewed the life of everyone who believes in your name. Bless my life with the healing presence of Peter and the belief of Thomas so that I can be a living sign of risen life in the world.

Ask the risen Lord to help you trust in him completely as you continue to pray.

CONTEMPLATIO

Peter brought healing to the lives of others because he was so transformed by the presence of the risen Christ within him. Contemplate the Spirit of Jesus within Peter, and open your heart to allow God to bless you with the spiritual gifts of peace and joy.

OPERATIO

Peter became a powerful instrument of Jesus' healing presence for others through the gifts of peace, joy, and the Holy Spirit that he received from the risen Lord. What can you do to manifest these gifts and share more fully in the mission of Jesus?

Third Sunday of Easter

LECTIO

Light a candle, or place some other symbol before you to focus your attention. As you read, feel free to highlight, underline, circle, or mark up the text and commentary as a tool for interacting with the readings. Vocalize the words of the text so that you not only read with your eyes but hear with your ears.

ACTS 5:27-32, 40B-41

When the captain and the court officers had brought the apostles in and made them stand before the Sanhedrin, the high priest questioned them, "We gave you strict orders, did we not, to stop teaching in that name? Yet you have filled Jerusalem with your teaching and want to bring this man's blood upon us." But Peter and the apostles said in reply, "We must obey God rather than men. The God of our ancestors raised Jesus, though you had him killed by hanging him on a tree. God exalted him at his right hand as leader and savior to grant Israel repentance and forgiveness of sins. We are witnesses of these things, as is the Holy Spirit whom God has given to those who obey him."

The Sanhedrin ordered the apostles to stop speaking in the name of Jesus, and dismissed them. So they left the presence of the Sanhedrin, rejoicing that they had been found worthy to suffer dishonor for the sake of the name.

⋏

The difference the resurrection made in the lives of Jesus' first disciples is evident in this scene from Jerusalem. Peter, who had denied even knowing Jesus before his death, emerges as the fearless leader of the Church and a courageous witness to the resurrection of Jesus. Willing now to suffer and die for the sake of the gospel, his life illustrates the power of forgiveness and the transformation that faith offers.

The dramatic narrative illustrates how the gospel cannot be contained. The greater the efforts made by the religious authorities to prevent the apostles from teaching in the name of Jesus, the more effective their witness becomes. Called in before the Sanhedrin, Peter and the apostles refuse to obey their order to be silent about Jesus. Ordered to cease preaching, Peter defiantly responds, "We must obey God rather than men" (Acts 5:29).

The experience of the Lord's resurrection implies a vocation to evangelize, to pass on to others the good news. So the apostles make it plain to the authorities who persecute them that they have no option other than to place their divine calling before all other human commands and prohibitions. This same pattern continues for the Church throughout history. The more the Church is silenced, oppressed, and persecuted, the more it grows and the stronger it becomes.

As Acts demonstrates throughout, the gospel cannot be contained because the witness of believers is joined with that of the Spirit. As the apostles declare, "We are witnesses of these things, as is the Holy Spirit whom God has given to those who obey him" (Acts 5:32). The Spirit transforms those who follow Jesus, their way of life, their outlook on the future, their relationship with one another, and their priorities. The Holy Spirit who fills their lives is the witness that confirms the human witnesses and shows that their work is the work of God.

JOHN 21:1-19

At that time, Jesus revealed himself again to his disciples at the Sea of Tiberias. He revealed himself in this way. Together were Simon Peter, Thomas called Didymus, Nathanael from Cana in Galilee, Zebedee's sons, and two others of his disciples. Simon Peter said to them, "I am going fishing." They said to him, "We also will come with you." So they went out and got into the boat, but that night they caught nothing. When it was already dawn, Jesus was standing on the shore; but the disciples did not realize that it was Jesus. Jesus said to them, "Children, have you caught anything to eat?" They answered him, "No." So he said to them, "Cast the net over the right side of the boat and you will find something." So they cast it, and were not able to pull it in because of the number of fish. So the disciple whom Jesus loved said to Peter, "It is the Lord." When Simon Peter heard that it was the Lord, he tucked in his garment, for he was lightly clad, and jumped into the sea. The other disciples came in the boat, for they were not far from shore, only about a hundred yards, dragging the net with the fish. When they climbed out on shore, they saw a charcoal fire with fish on it and bread. Jesus said to them, "Bring some of the fish you just caught." So Simon Peter went over and dragged the net ashore full of one hundred fifty-three large fish. Even though there were so many, the net was not torn. Jesus said to them, "Come, have breakfast." And none of the disciples dared to ask him, "Who are you?" because they realized it was the Lord. Jesus came over and took the bread and gave it to them, and in like manner the fish. This was now the third time Jesus was revealed to his disciples after being raised from the dead.

When they had finished breakfast, Jesus said to Simon Peter, "Simon, son of John, do you love me more than these?" Simon Peter answered him, "Yes, Lord, you know that I love you." Jesus said to him, "Feed my lambs." He then said to Simon Peter a second time, "Simon, son of John, do you love me?" Simon Peter answered him, "Yes, Lord, you know that I love you." Jesus said to him, "Tend my sheep." Jesus said to him the third time, "Simon, son of John, do you love me?" Peter was distressed that Jesus had said to him a third time, "Do you love me?" and he said to him, "Lord, you know everything; you know that I love you." Jesus said to him, "Feed my sheep. Amen, amen, I say to you, when you were younger, you used to dress yourself and go where you wanted; but when you grow old, you will stretch out your hands, and someone else will dress you and lead you where you do not want to go." He said this signifying by what kind of death he would glorify God. And when he had said this, he said to him, "Follow me."

人

Peter and six other disciples have gathered back in Galilee after the traumatic events of Jesus' final days in Jerusalem. They venture out on the sea they know so well for a night of fishing. But after fishing in the dark and catching nothing, they follow the commands of Jesus in the morning light and draw in an abundant catch. We are drawn into a scene full of rich symbolism, and we may step into the shoes of the seventh disciple, who remains anonymous. These seven, the number of completeness, represent the community of believers throughout the centuries who encounter the risen Lord, let down their nets to evangelize humanity, eat with him, and follow in his way.

As Peter plunges into the water, we are reminded that the way to the risen Lord is through the water of baptism. As Peter joins with the other disciples to share a meal with the Lord, we recall our invitation to share his presence in the Eucharist. And we realize that the natural consequence of baptism and Eucharist is the commission by Jesus to share in his mission.

Through the eyes of Peter, we can experience the transforming work of Jesus. By making a charcoal fire, Jesus reminds Peter of the dark scene of his denial in the high priest's courtyard. But how different these burning coals must have looked to Peter in the light of dawn as Jesus prepares a meal of communion and reconciliation upon them. In the presence of this new fire, which is warm and inviting, Jesus offers Peter another chance to affirm his discipleship. As Peter had three times denied his relationship with Jesus, now Jesus gives Peter this threefold opportunity to express his love for him.

Jesus ends his commissioning of Peter with the same words that began their relationship: "Follow me" (John 21:19). Peter will follow Jesus now with new understanding. Stripped of his vain pride and self-reliance, Peter is now able to love with fidelity and commitment because he has failed and been forgiven. The love of a disciple is costly and sacrificial. "You will stretch out your hands," Jesus tells Peter (21:18). He will stretch out his hands in service, in prayer, and, finally, on the cross of martyrdom. As fisherman and shepherd of the Church, Peter is a model of faith and love for all believers.

MEDITATIO

Experience the transforming power of God's word as you place yourself within these scenes and learn from the risen Lord.

- Why is it impossible to silence or oppress the good news of Jesus Christ? Why do attempts to contain the gospel usually have the opposite effect?

- Peter is transformed from someone who denied Jesus at his passion to someone who now courageously witnesses to his resurrection and is willing to suffer and die for him. What does Peter teach you about being a disciple and serving his Church?

- Use your imagination to enter the Gospel scene on the shore of the sea. What are the sights and sounds, the aromas, the tastes and textures that come alive as you imagine yourself there with Jesus? What are you thinking and feeling?

- What might be some of the emotions Peter felt when he saw the charcoal fire that Jesus had prepared on the shore of the sea? What are you learning from Jesus' way of offering healing and forgiveness to Peter?

- Before commissioning Peter for service, Jesus did not ask about his talents, his strengths, or his endurance. He asked only if Peter's love for him was supreme. Why is love for Jesus the most important qualification for a disciple of Christ?

ORATIO

After listening and reflecting on the word of God, respond to that word with your whole heart, mind, body, and soul. Begin with this prayer, and continue to pray as your heart directs you:

Risen Lord, bring your light into my darkness, your power to my frailties, and your forgiveness to my failures. Give me the insight to recognize your presence and the courage to follow you. Help me to love you more so that I can accomplish the mission you give to me this day.

Continue praying with whatever words arise from your loving union with Jesus.

CONTEMPLATIO

Picture yourself in the warm sunshine on the seashore with Jesus. Rest in his presence and soak in the healing forgiveness and nourishment he offers to you.

OPERATIO

Through the resurrection of Jesus, the same power and courage given to Peter are available to all Christians. In the Holy Spirit, we are given a desire to say and do things that we might previously have felt were impossible for us. What are you being empowered or transformed to say or do during this week of Easter?

Fourth Sunday of Easter

LECTIO

Λ

In a comfortable and quiet place of prayer, close off the distractions of the day and enter a moment of stillness. Ask God's Spirit to fill your heart and guide your listening. Open yourself to whatever new insight or encouragement God wishes to offer you.

ACTS 13:14, 43-52

Paul and Barnabas continued on from Perga and reached Antioch in Pisidia. On the sabbath they entered the synagogue and took their seats. Many Jews and worshipers who were converts to Judaism followed Paul and Barnabas, who spoke to them and urged them to remain faithful to the grace of God.

On the following sabbath almost the whole city gathered to hear the word of the Lord. When the Jews saw the crowds, they were filled with jealousy and with violent abuse contradicted what Paul said. Both Paul and Barnabas spoke out boldly and said, "It was necessary that the word of God be spoken to you first, but since you reject it and condemn yourselves as unworthy of eternal life, we now turn to the Gentiles. For so the Lord has commanded us,

I have made you a light to the Gentiles,
that you may be an instrument of salvation
to the ends of the earth."

The Gentiles were delighted when they heard this and glorified the word of the Lord. All who were destined for eternal life came to believe, and the word of the Lord continued to spread through the whole region. The Jews, however, incited the women of prominence who were worshipers and the leading men of the city, stirred up a persecution against Paul and Barnabas, and expelled them from their territory. So they shook the dust from their feet in protest against them, and went to Iconium. The disciples were filled with joy and the Holy Spirit.

On his missionary journeys, Paul preaches from town to town, going first to the synagogues on the Sabbath. Repeatedly, Paul's preaching of the good news of Jesus, connected with the Scriptures of Israel, is called "the word of the Lord." He and Barnabas draw large crowds of both Jews and Gentiles; in fact, Luke notes here that "almost the whole city gathered to hear the word of the Lord" (Acts 13:44). This positive reception by so many causes some of the Jewish leaders to be stirred to jealousy because the Gentiles are being invited to share the faith of Israel. They contradict Paul, reject his inclusive message, and begin to stir up a persecution.

In response, Paul speaks out boldly, demonstrating how his mission from the Lord is a response to the words of Isaiah: "I have made you a light to the Gentiles, / that you may be an instrument of salvation / to the ends of the earth" (Acts 13:47). This ancient prophecy of God's saving plan for the nations is fulfilled in Jesus and extended through his Church and the work of Paul. God has commanded Barnabas and Paul to be a guiding light to the nations concerning the way to God. The goal of God's plan is to take the message of salvation in Jesus Christ to the ends of the earth, to extend it to all nations in every part of the world.

From this point on, Paul turns increasingly to the Gentiles, although he never turns his back on the people of Israel. In nearly every city of his travels, he goes first to the Jews, and when turned away by one synagogue, he goes to another. He knows that the covenant benefits were promised first to his own people, and he never ceases to identify himself with them. Yet he is also the apostle to the Gentiles, called to bring the message of salvation to all the nations of the earth.

JOHN 10:27-30

Jesus said: "My sheep hear my voice; I know them, and they follow me. I give them eternal life, and they shall never perish. No one can take them out of my hand. My Father, who has given them to me, is greater than all, and no one can take them out of the Father's hand. The Father and I are one."

⋏

This unusually brief Gospel reading, selected from the larger discourse of Jesus in which he declares that he is the Good Shepherd, conveys a great deal in just a few words. The imagery of the shepherd and the sheep evokes all the pastoral images throughout the psalms, the prophets, and the history of Israel. The patriarchs of Israel herded their flocks, and Moses was drawn to the burning bush while herding sheep. David was a shepherd of sheep before he became Israel's king. It is not surprising that the poets of Israel would think of their God as the shepherd who neither slumbers nor sleeps but is always protecting and guiding his people.

Those who lived in the pastoral environment of the ancient world knew that there was a close relationship between sheep and shepherd, a bond of trust and affection. They knew the total dedication of shepherds to their sheep, who perhaps even risked their lives to defend the flock from a wild beast or to rescue those stranded in out-of-the-way places. The ancients knew the way the shepherd led his flock through his presence and his voice, calling his sheep to follow, guiding them to those distant oases where there is fresh grazing and flowing water.

Jesus' portrayal of his sheep is a description of authentic believers: they listen to the voice of Jesus and they follow him; Jesus knows them and leads them to eternal life; and no one can snatch them away from him. These pastoral images describe the intimacy of the relationship between Jesus and his disciples as well as Jesus' complete and unconditional dedication to them.

Jesus knows that the close and tender relationship that he shares with his disciples reflects the intimate bond he has with the Father. As Jesus says, "The Father and I are one" (John 10:30). To be guided by Jesus is to be led by the Father into life in its fullness. Because Jesus and the Father are one, disciples belong equally to the Father, who protects and cares for them. Through faith the disciples are joined to Jesus, who is united with the Father. The shepherd guides the sheep to streams and pastures—ultimately, life with God forever.

MEDITATIO

人

Spend some time reflecting on the Scripture passages you have read, allowing them to interact with your own world of memories, questions, ideas, and concerns until you are aware of the personal messages the texts offer to you.

- How does the verse from Isaiah 49:6 that is quoted by St. Paul in Acts 13:47 describe Paul's mission? How does it describe the mission of the Church today?

- The scene from Acts shows a variety of emotional responses created by "the word of the Lord" (13:44) spoken through Paul among the various groups in the city. Why does Paul's message produce such a variety of reactions? What are the responses generated by the word of the Lord today?

- Paul and Barnabas are "filled with joy and the Holy Spirit" (Acts 13:52), traveling from city to city, despite the rejection and persecution they experience. What does their lack of discouragement indicate about their mission? How is it possible to avoid discouragement when doing the work of the Lord?

- The pastoral images of John's Gospel describe the Christian life through the imagery of shepherd and sheep.

In what ways do these verses describe your experience of following Jesus?

- The word of the Lord is the voice of the Shepherd. In what ways is your practice of lectio divina helping you to hear God's voice in the Scriptures?

ORATIO

After listening to the word of the Lord through your reading and reflection, respond to God through the words of your prayer. You may wish to begin with these words:

Saving Lord, you have raised up Jesus your Son to be the light for all the nations so that your salvation will come to all peoples. Help me to listen carefully to your word so that I may be a bearer of your gospel in the world.

Continue expressing your heart to the Father who knows you intimately, cares about you deeply, and accepts you unconditionally.

CONTEMPLATIO

Listen to the reassuring words of Jesus: "My sheep hear my voice; I know them, and they follow me" (John 10:27). As you contemplate these words in silence, allow yourself to become increasingly confident and trusting in the voice of Jesus as you continue to follow him.

OPERATIO

"A light to the Gentiles" and "an instrument of salvation to the ends of the earth" (Acts 13:47) describe the mission of Jesus and his extended mission in his Church. How does your life fit into that mission? How can you reach out of your comfort zone to bring light to a person or situation in need of God's grace this week?

Fifth Sunday of Easter

LECTIO

Call upon the renewing Spirit of God to enlighten your eyes and your mind as you prepare to read the inspired Scriptures. Open yourself to whatever new insight or encouragement God wishes to offer you.

ACTS 14:21-27

After Paul and Barnabas had proclaimed the good news to that city and made a considerable number of disciples, they returned to Lystra and to Iconium and to Antioch. They strengthened the spirits of the disciples and exhorted them to persevere in the faith, saying, "It is necessary for us to undergo many hardships to enter the kingdom of God." They appointed elders for them in each church and, with prayer and fasting, commended them to the Lord in whom they had put their faith. Then they traveled through Pisidia and reached Pamphylia. After proclaiming the word at Perga they went down to Attalia. From there they sailed to Antioch, where they had been commended to the grace of God for the work they had now accomplished. And when they arrived, they called the church together and reported what God had done with them and how he had opened the door of faith to the Gentiles.

⋀

The billions of Christians who form the worldwide Church today descend from a few thousand scattered throughout the Roman Empire of the first century. The thousands of dioceses that constitute the Church today are the heirs of the few dozen local churches founded or visited by Paul and Barnabas in the ancient Mediterranean world. Thanks to the committed zeal of people like Paul and Barnabas and their co-workers, these early communities received a firm foundation and expanded to become the global Church of our day. Acts offers us a breathless recital of the journeys of these missionaries from city to city as they exhorted the local churches and encouraged them to persevere in the faith despite many hardships.

In their planting and nurturing of new communities, the apostles were convinced that God's grace was inspiring and empowering them. Their example of suffering for the faith and perseverance in the mission inspired the communities and gave credibility to their leadership. Discerning the need to stabilize the young churches with local leadership, they wisely appointed "elders," or presbyters, in each community, but only after prayer and fasting (Acts 14:23). They entrusted them to the Lord, confident that they would carry on the work after the apostles had departed.

On returning to Antioch and to the community that had sent them on their mission, Paul and Barnabas reported "what God had done with them" (Acts 14:27). They knew they were not individual adventurists, but apostles. They had been sent out, commissioned as God's instruments to communicate the good news of Jesus Christ far and wide. And they gladly reported that God had "opened the door of faith to the Gentiles" (14:27) through their mission.

JOHN 13:31-33A, 34-35

When Judas had left them, Jesus said, "Now is the Son of Man glorified, and God is glorified in him. If God is glorified in him, God will also glorify him in himself, and God will glorify him at once. My children, I will be with you only a little while longer. I give you a new commandment: love one another. As I have loved you, so you also should love one another. This is how all will know that you are my disciples, if you have love for one another."

The Gospel presents us with the opening words of Jesus' long farewell discourse. These final words of Jesus to his disciples are his personal and mystical exploration of the meaning and implications of his death and resurrection for his followers. Addressing his disciples tenderly as "my children" (John 13:33), Jesus emphasizes two verbs, "glorify" and "love," and repeats them several times in different forms.

In speaking of his death on the cross and his resurrection, Jesus says, "Now is the Son of Man glorified, and God is glorified in him" (John 13:31). His darkest hour is transformed into his glorification. Throughout the Bible, the word "glory" signifies a visible manifestation of God's presence to his people. In the Old Testament, the glory of the Lord was experienced in fire, cloud, and a host of other tangible appearances. As Jesus prepares for the climax of his life, the truth of his life as a manifestation of the Father will be made clear. When he is lifted up in crucifixion as the ultimate and perfect sign of God's love for us, his glorification will be accomplished.

Before Jesus departs from his disciples, he gives them a "new" commandment: "Love one another" (John 13:34). There is really nothing new about this instruction; the Old Testament is filled with directives to love God and neighbor. The command is new because it comes directly from Jesus, who offers his own sacrificial love as the model: "As I have loved you, so you also should love one another" (13:34). In biblical language, love is not just a feeling toward another, but consists of visible acts for others that bespeak selfless commitment and sacrifice. To love as Jesus taught, it is necessary to act toward the other in the way Jesus acted as he washed the feet of his disciples and gave himself totally on the cross. Sometimes loving feelings result from loving actions extended and received, but the essence of love is action that is rooted in God's love for us.

Jesus emphasizes the witness aspect of his command to love. One of the most striking and attractive features of early Christianity was the love its members showed to one another. It made outsiders inquire about what these people believed and why they acted as they did. Disciples of Jesus expressing their love for God and others in what they do—this remains the most eloquent sign to the world and the most effective way to evangelize.

MEDITATIO

⋀

- Jesus' new commandment to love as he loves was incarnated by the early Christians and is illustrated by the ministry of Paul and Barnabas. What characteristics of the apostles' ministry among the churches are most inspiring to you?

- Through the faith and zeal of the apostles, the Church grew rapidly from its small beginnings in Jerusalem. What do you suppose were some of the reasons for its rapid growth throughout the Roman Empire?

- What lessons can our Church today learn from Paul and Barnabas and their co-workers?

- Count how many times a variation of the verb "glorify" is used in the Gospel reading. As Jesus is glorified in his death and resurrection, God is glorified in him. How does Jesus manifest God's glory to the world?

- If the standard of Christian love is the love with which Jesus has loved us, what are some of the characteristics of this love? How have Jesus' acts of love toward you empowered you to love others?

ORATIO

⋏

Respond to God's word with your own words of prayer. Include the ideas, images, and vocabulary of Scripture to enrich the content of your prayer. Use this prayer for a starter:

Glorious Lord, you love us totally and completely, and you instruct us to love one another with this love. Teach me to rid my life of selfishness and to love sacrificially and generously. Give me the grace to love others as you love me.

Continue to pray as your heart directs you.

CONTEMPLATIO

⋏

Hold in your hands or evoke in your imagination an image of the cross. Consider the sacrificial and unconditional love of God for you that this image represents. Let that love fill your heart and transform you to offer that kind of love to others.

OPERATIO

⋏

Jesus does not envision his Church as a closed circle of mutually exchanged love, but one that keeps widening outward. Just as Paul and Barnabas energetically traversed Asia Minor, offering the good news even to Gentiles, so the commandment to love demands that we continue to open our circle of faith to others. What can I do this week to love expansively and unselfishly as Jesus has commanded?

Sixth Sunday of Easter

LECTIO

On this Sunday before the Ascension, the readings focus on Jesus' departure and his promise of the Holy Spirit. Ask the Holy Spirit to help you listen and respond to the *sacra pagina* and to work within you, as the Spirit guided the apostles to listen and respond to the word of the Lord.

When you have quieted your external and internal distractions, dedicate this time for sacred conversation with God.

ACTS 15:1-2, 22-29

Some who had come down from Judea were instructing the brothers, "Unless you are circumcised according to the Mosaic practice, you cannot be saved." Because there arose no little dissension and debate by Paul and Barnabas with them, it was decided that Paul, Barnabas, and some of the others should go up to Jerusalem to the apostles and elders about this question.

The apostles and elders, in agreement with the whole church, decided to choose representatives and to send them to Antioch with Paul and Barnabas. The ones chosen were Judas, who was called Barsabbas, and Silas, leaders among the brothers. This is the letter delivered by them:

"The apostles and the elders, your brothers, to the brothers in Antioch, Syria, and Cilicia of Gentile origin: greetings.

Since we have heard that some of our number who went out without any mandate from us have upset you with their teachings and disturbed your peace of mind, we have with one accord decided to choose representatives and to send them to you along with our beloved Barnabas and Paul, who have dedicated their lives to the name of our Lord Jesus Christ. So we are sending Judas and Silas who will also convey this same message by word of mouth: 'It is the decision of the Holy Spirit and of us not to place on you any burden beyond these necessities, namely, to abstain from meat sacrificed to idols, from blood, from meats of strangled animals, and from unlawful marriage. If you keep free of these, you will be doing what is right. Farewell.'"

The work of the Holy Spirit in the life of the Church is both conservative and progressive. The Spirit helps the Church conserve and safeguard its memory of Jesus, his teachings, and the Scriptures that anticipated his coming. The Spirit also helps the Church progress into the future, bringing new understanding and experience of the paschal mystery into every age of history.

This episode from the early Church demonstrates the working of the Holy Spirit at a momentous time of decision for the apostles. The question that faced them was whether Gentiles needed to become Jews as they accepted Jesus into their lives and became Christians. The Church had begun as a small sect within Judaism. The first followers of Jesus regarded their movement as a new and complete way of being Jewish. However, when Gentiles began to respond to the apostles and to receive the Holy Spirit, there were strong opinions on both sides about whether these Gentiles needed to undergo circumcision and observe the Jewish laws pertaining to the Sabbath rest, food, and ritual purity.

A group from Judea, not authorized by the Jerusalem apostles, came to Antioch, where Paul and Barnabas were recounting all that God was doing through them in their missionary travels among the Gentiles. These Judeans argued for full observance of the law by Gentile converts, while Paul and Barnabas held that Gentiles should not be bound by the Mosaic practices. When the apostles and elders in Jerusalem reached an agreement on this matter, they sent an apostolic letter along with their own representatives to the Gentile churches being served by Paul and Barnabas. The letter stated that Gentiles did not need to become Jews and observe the Law of Moses except in four matters. These exceptions would allow observant Jewish converts to share table fellowship with the new Gentile Christians.

By prefacing their letter with a statement that the Church's decision was a result of the apostles' discernment and "the decision of the Holy Spirit" (Acts 15:28), the leaders acknowledged how the gift of the Spirit is alive in the Church. They affirmed the primacy of the Holy Spirit in guiding and governing the Christian movement. Since the Gentiles were already receiving the Holy Spirit, the Holy Spirit had effectively solved the problem. The work of the Holy Spirit was conserving the essentials of Jesus' teachings and example, and also leading the Church into a future directed beyond Israel to the whole world.

John 14:23-29

Jesus said to his disciples: "Whoever loves me will keep my word, and my Father will love him, and we will come to him and make our dwelling with him. Whoever does not love me does not keep my words; yet the word you hear is not mine but that of the Father who sent me.

"I have told you this while I am with you. The Advocate, the Holy Spirit, whom the Father will send in my name, will teach you everything and remind you of all that I told you. Peace I leave with you; my peace I give to you. Not as the world gives do I give it to you. Do not let your hearts be troubled or afraid. You heard me tell you, 'I am going away and I will come back to you.' If you loved me, you would rejoice that I am going to the Father; for the Father is greater than I. And now I have told you this before it happens, so that when it happens you may believe."

Although Jesus is departing from his disciples to return to the Father, he does not leave them alone. He promises to send his Holy Spirit to them, the Spirit of truth, the Spirit of peace, the Advocate who will be forever by their side. The Holy Spirit is a gift from God, but a gift that must be accepted through our loving, active response to God's word. Through the Spirit, Jesus and the Father will make their home in us forever.

Although Jesus taught his followers many things throughout his ministry with them on earth, they were unable to understand much of what he told them because the heart of his truth would be revealed in his death and resurrection. Jesus tells his disciples that the role of the Holy Spirit is to "teach you everything and remind you of all that I told you" (John 14:26). The Spirit of truth will continue the teaching of Jesus and deepen within his disciples the transforming reality of his dying and rising. The Spirit will enable believers to experience Jesus days, years, and centuries after his earthly life.

The effect of the Holy Spirit's work within believers is a profound sense of peace. The *shalom* that Jesus gives is not complacent, sentimental, or passive. It comforts the afflicted, but it also afflicts the comfortable. Jesus says to his disciples, "My peace I give to you" (John 14:27), the kind of peace that the world cannot give. The *pax Romana* (Roman peace), secured by the emperor Augustus during the lifetime of Jesus, was obtained and maintained by military might. The peace given by Jesus, in contrast, was not obtained by inflicting violence, nor was it maintained with force. This peace of the Lord is the right relationship that flows from our loving union with God through Jesus and the Holy Spirit. This is the peace that lasts, the peace that does not go away even in the midst of life's most difficult struggles.

MEDITATIO

Reflect on these Scriptures from the midst of your own hopes and longings. Consider Jesus' promises to you and how God wishes to dwell within you.

- By leading the Church of the first century to accept Gentiles into its fellowship, the Holy Spirit moved the community to become a global Church. How does the Holy Spirit continue to lead the Church of the twenty-first century to continue this process?

- The decision made by the apostles was not simply a wise compromise or the product of effective strategic planning. Rather than being a democratic process, it was called by the apostles "the decision of the Holy Spirit and of us" (Acts 15:28). What are some of the principles involved in this apostolic decision making?

- The Acts of the Apostles indicates that the early Church was never free of tensions and that dissension and debate were important elements in personal and communal discernment. What lessons can you learn from the apostles about solving problems and resolving disputes peacefully?

- The risen Jesus offers the gift of his own peace to us. In what sense is this peace both freely given and yet costly in its demands? How do you experience the peace that Jesus leaves with you?

- Before his departure from his disciples, Jesus prepares them for life in the age of the Spirit. What are some of the changes the Church experiences after his departure? In what sense is the work of the Spirit both conservative and progressive in the Church?

ORATIO

⅄

Pray for the gift of the Holy Spirit as Jesus instructed his disciples to pray. Speak the words that help you respond to the word of God that you have heard. You may begin with these:

Glorified Christ, you promise to give me peace when I am troubled and confused. Send me you Spirit of truth to continue your revealing work and to live in me always. Make your dwelling within me through the gift of the Holy Spirit.

Continue to pray in your own words from your heart.

CONTEMPLATIO

⅄

When the words of prayer are no longer necessary or helpful, just rest silently and confidently, trusting that the Spirit of God fills your heart, giving you the peace that God alone can offer.

OPERATIO

⅄

At the sign of peace in the liturgy, the priest repeats the words of Jesus from the Gospel: "Peace I leave you; my peace I give to you" (John 14:27). We pray that God will give peace and unity to the Church in accordance with his will. What does your reflection on these Scriptures add to the gesture you offer those around you this Sunday in the sign of peace?

The Ascension of the Lord

LECTIO

Λ

Luke addressed both his Gospel and the Acts of the Apostles to Theophilus, yet he also addressed his words to all who would read this text through the ages. Realize that Luke is addressing these words personally to you and that God is speaking to you through the divine word of Sacred Scripture.

When you have quieted your external and internal distractions, dedicate this time for sacred conversation with God.

ACTS 1:1-11

In the first book, Theophilus, I dealt with all that Jesus did and taught until the day he was taken up, after giving instructions through the Holy Spirit to the apostles whom he had chosen. He presented himself alive to them by many proofs after he had suffered, appearing to them during forty days and speaking about the kingdom of God. While meeting with them, he enjoined them not to depart from Jerusalem, but to wait for "the promise of the Father about which you have heard me speak; for John baptized with water, but in a few days you will be baptized with the Holy Spirit."

When they had gathered together they asked him, "Lord, are you at this time going to restore the kingdom to Israel?" He answered them, "It is not for you to know the times or seasons that the Father has established by his own authority.

But you will receive power when the Holy Spirit comes upon you, and you will be my witnesses in Jerusalem, throughout Judea and Samaria, and to the ends of the earth." When he had said this, as they were looking on, he was lifted up, and a cloud took him from their sight. While they were looking intently at the sky as he was going, suddenly two men dressed in white garments stood beside them. They said, "Men of Galilee, why are you standing there looking at the sky? This Jesus who has been taken up from you into heaven will return in the same way as you have seen him going into heaven."

The Acts of the Apostles begins where the Gospel of Luke ends. At the end of his Gospel, Luke says that Jesus blessed his disciples, parted from them, "and was taken up to heaven" (24:51). In the Gospel, Luke emphasizes that Jesus' ascension into heaven marks the close of Jesus' earthly ministry and the establishment of his heavenly reign. In Acts, Luke stresses that Jesus' ascension marks the beginning of the Church's mission. What the Ascension marks, then, is both an ending and a beginning, the last impression of Jesus in the Gospel and the inauguration of his rule over his Church until he comes again.

At the beginning of his Gospel, Luke describes a period of "forty days" (4:2) in which Jesus prepares for his public ministry after his baptism, as he is led by the Holy Spirit into the desert. At the beginning of Acts, Luke describes another period of "forty days" in which the disciples prepare before they are "baptized with the Holy Spirit" (1:3, 5) and begin their public witnessing to the resurrected Christ. During those forty days, Jesus gave his apostles fuller instructions about the reign of God. "Forty days" recalls the experience of the two ancestors who spoke with Jesus on the mountain of transfiguration. For forty days, God instructed Moses in the law on Mount Sinai; for forty days, Elijah journeyed to the same mountain before his encounter with God in the "silent sound" (1 Kings 19:12). Forty always marks a transition to something new, often to a new stage of God's saving plan: from Jesus' wilderness experience to his public ministry; from the earthly presence of Jesus to his presence in the Spirit in the life of the Church.

The Ascension is one aspect of the broader mystery of the resurrection. Because Jesus is no longer bodily present among his disciples, the Church is now living in a new reality. Throughout the earlier Sundays of Easter, the Scriptures showed Jesus assuring his followers that they were truly experiencing his real presence. The Scriptures of the Ascension focus on Jesus' exaltation. We behold him in all his divine glory, taking his place in heaven, seated next to his Father in his heavenly reign.

It is not enough for his disciples to stand awestruck looking heavenward. They must wait and pray for the coming of the Holy Spirit ,who will enable them to be his witnesses "to the ends of the earth" (Acts 1:8). As we celebrate the Ascension, we must realize that we, too, are called to be a Church of witnesses. Yet we are not expected to begin our task by our own power or expertise. We, too, must wait and pray; then we will be able to redirect our gaze from the heavens to the earthbound task that awaits us.

LUKE 24:46-53

Jesus said to his disciples: "Thus it is written that the Christ would suffer and rise from the dead on the third day and that repentance, for the forgiveness of sins, would be preached in his name to all the nations, beginning from Jerusalem. You are witnesses of these things. And behold I am sending the promise of my Father upon you; but stay in the city until you are clothed with power from on high."

Then he led them out as far as Bethany, raised his hands, and blessed them. As he blessed them he parted from them and was taken up to heaven. They did him homage and then returned to Jerusalem with great joy, and they were continually in the temple praising God.

At the conclusion of Luke's Gospel, Jesus again opens his disciples' eyes and hearts to the unfolding of God's saving plan. Jesus explains what he says is written in the ancient Scriptures: that the Messiah would suffer and rise from the dead and that a message of repentance and forgiveness would be proclaimed to all nations as a result. The first two of these elements of God's plan have just been completed, the suffering and resurrection of Christ, and the last part remains for the disciples to carry out. Jesus then commissions his disciples for the decisive role they are to play in the new and final phase of salvation history: they are to be his witnesses, proclaiming repentance and forgiveness, beginning in Jerusalem and extending to the whole world.

It is this witness of the disciples that is the subject of Luke's second volume, the Acts of the Apostles. The goal of Jesus' journey to Jerusalem now becomes the starting point from which the message of salvation will extend to the ends of the earth. But this witness is not only the purpose of the apostles' mission of so long ago; it is also the vocation of all disciples down through the ages. Extending the good news of Jesus the Savior is the mission of all believers from the ascension of Jesus to his return in glory at the end of time.

The Gospel concludes with Jesus' promise to send the Holy Spirit and the ascension of Jesus to the Father. Although his resurrection appearances have come to an end, the Church will continue to experience his glorified presence and activity in many ways. As the Gospel closes, the disciples are left waiting in Jerusalem for what God will do next. As we celebrate the Ascension of Jesus, we, too, wait for God's next move and for God's Spirit-filled empowerment for our mission in the world.

MEDITATIO

Reflect on the end of Luke's Gospel and the beginning of his Acts of the Apostles, realizing that the end is a new beginning. Let these Scriptures touch your heart by your meditation in light of your own experiences of trust and hope.

- In Luke's resurrection account, two men in dazzling garments ask the women at the tomb, "Why do you seek the living one among the dead?" (24:5). In Luke's ascension account, as the disciples are witnessing Jesus being taken up in a cloud from their sight, the two men dressed in white garments ask them, "Why are you standing there looking at the sky?" (Acts 1:11). What is the relationship between these two questions?

- The number forty is used throughout Scripture to indicate a time of transition, from one stage of God's plan to another. What is the deeper significance of the forty days leading from the resurrection to the ascension of Jesus?

- In Luke's Gospel, the ascension of Jesus is an ending; in Acts, the ascension is a beginning. How and why does Luke present the ascension differently in each of his writings?

- In what ways is the Church a witness to Jesus Christ in the world today? How is your life a part of that witness?

- In what sense is Luke's Gospel incomplete? What is necessary to complete it?

ORATIO

The angels urge the disciples not to remain gazing heavenward, but to look toward their mission in the world. Voice your response to the words you have heard in Scripture. You may begin with this prayer:

Risen Lord, send your Holy Spirit upon me so that I may be filled with joy and empowered to be your witness. Help me to recognize you as you make your presence known in word, sacrament, and the lives of your disciples today.

Continue to pray in your own words, seeking to imitate the faith of the original disciples of Jesus.

CONTEMPLATIO

At the end of the Gospel reading, Jesus says, "I am sending the promise of my Father upon you; but stay in the city until you are clothed with power from on high" (Luke 24:49). Spend some moments in silence, embodying the joyful expectation and confident trust of the disciples in Jerusalem.

OPERATIO

At the end of the Gospel reading, Jesus says, "I am sending
As you anticipate Pentecost during these remaining days of the Easter season, take away the obstacles that might prevent the Holy Spirit from filling your heart and manifesting the divine presence in your life. What form will this preparation take in your life?

Seventh Sunday of Easter

LECTIO

Open your heart and allow the Spirit of God to lead you through this lectio divina, guide your understanding, and kindle within you the fire of divine love.

Begin reading when you feel ready to hear God's voice speaking in Scripture. Slowly articulate the words so that you can listen better as you read.

ACTS 7:55-60

Stephen, filled with the Holy Spirit, looked up intently to heaven and saw the glory of God and Jesus standing at the right hand of God, and Stephen said, "Behold, I see the heavens opened and the Son of Man standing at the right hand of God." But they cried out in a loud voice, covered their ears, and rushed upon him together. They threw him out of the city, and began to stone him. The witnesses laid down their cloaks at the feet of a young man named Saul. As they were stoning Stephen, he called out, "Lord Jesus, receive my spirit." Then he fell to his knees and cried out in a loud voice, "Lord, do not hold this sin against them"; and when he said this, he fell asleep.

The narrative of Stephen in the Acts of the Apostles forms an important link between the Gospel accounts of Jesus and the life of the early Church. In recounting the entire witness of Stephen, the author demonstrates how he is both a follower and an imitator of Jesus. Like Jesus, Stephen is accused of blasphemy and false witnesses testify against him; like Jesus, he is condemned to death and taken outside the city to be executed; like Jesus, he prays for forgiveness for his slayers; and just as Jesus delivered over his spirit to the Father, so Stephen in his final moments commits his spirit to Jesus. The parallels are made explicit in order to make the point that disciples are called to follow in the footsteps of Jesus as his witnesses in the world. As an imitator of Jesus, Stephen forms a particular example of the way the ministry of Jesus is reflected and continued in his Church.

Stephen is known as the first martyr of the Church because he died as the consequence of his bold profession of Christian faith. He faced his death, in imitation of Jesus, with courage and compassion. The word "martyr" derives from the Greek word for "witness." Stephen gave witness to the Lord's death and resurrection in a supreme manner by giving his life to the end. He is the first in a long and glorious line of martyrs in the Church, a heavenly assembly whose numbers continue to grow today.

At the moment of his death, Stephen's faith enabled him to see beyond his horrible circumstances and experience a vision demonstrating his intimate relationship with the Trinity. Stephen was "filled with the Holy Spirit," and he "saw the glory of God and Jesus standing at the right hand of God" (Acts 7:55). Stephen's murderers, by contrast, "covered their ears" (7:57) so that they would not hear the whispers of love emanating from God and radiating through Stephen. As disciples today, we must be able to see beyond the immediate historical circumstances of the Church in the world in order to understand how the Holy Spirit fills the Church and unites believers with the Father and with Jesus at his side in glory.

JOHN 17:20-26

Lifting up his eyes to heaven, Jesus prayed, saying: "Holy Father, I pray not only for them, but also for those who will believe in me through their word, so that they may all be one, as you, Father, are in me and I in you, that they also may be in us, that the world may believe that you sent me. And I have given them the glory you gave me, so that they may be one, as we are one, I in them and you in me, that they may be brought to perfection as one, that the world may know that you sent me, and that you loved them even as you loved me. Father, they are your gift to me. I wish that where I am they also may be with me, that they may see my glory that you gave me, because you loved me before the foundation of the world. Righteous Father, the world also does not know you, but I know you, and they know that you sent me. I made known to them your name and I will make it known, that the love with which you loved me may be in them and I in them."

$\wedge$

As Jesus voices his parting prayer to the Father, he prays, not only for the disciples gathered around him, but also for all future disciples who do not yet know him. His prayer includes all of us who will believe in Jesus through the word of his disciples. He prays for the unity of all disciples over the past twenty centuries, "that they may all be one" (John 17:21).

The oneness for which Jesus prays is not self-generated by the disciples. It is not first and foremost a social or organizational unity. It is, rather, rooted in the unity between God the Father and Jesus the Son. It is a deep unity established among believers as they are taken into the oneness of love that Jesus has shared eternally with the Father.

This unity is not only a source of fulfillment for believers, but it should be a powerful witness to the world. The unity that God has established between peoples through the resurrection of Christ—Jew and Gentile, rich and poor, male and female, slave and free person—is an effective evangelizing sign by which Christian faith may be spread. The oneness of many people from diverse lands and languages inspires people to seek the source and foundation of that unity.

The unity among disciples for which Jesus prays has nothing to do with uniformity. So often the Church settles for some kind of uniformity because genuine internal unity is so difficult to achieve. But the unity that comes through love for one another requires that individual people be true to their unique selves. Diversity, in fact, is the hallmark of a unified community. The genuine unity for which Jesus prayed is not a conformity of ideas but a community that is united in love, characterized by trust, and healed by forgiveness.

When the Church is united, it is able to give credible witness to the Father, who is united with the Son and the Spirit in revealing himself and in transmitting divine salvation to the world. United in the Father's love, the Church can express the same love with which the Father has loved the Son, and it can proclaim the good news of this love in a hostile world. In drawing us into his final prayer, Jesus asks that we who have experienced his love for the Father may accept our responsibility to draw others into the unity of love that constitutes the heart of the Trinity.

MEDITATIO

The challenge of meditatio is to continue reflecting on the Scriptures until they become a mirror in which we see our own reflection. Consider how the readings reflect the struggles, hopes, and desires of your own life.

- What is the significance of the parallelism between Luke's accounts of Jesus' death and Stephen's martyrdom? What does this text teach you about Christian death?

- Why are the martyrs of the Church such powerful witnesses to the gospel? Who is a martyr you admire from the Church's past centuries? Who would you consider to be a modern-day martyr?

- Within the narrative of Stephen's martyrdom, Luke briefly notes that "the witnesses laid down their cloaks at the feet of a young man named Saul" (Acts 7:58). This is Luke's first mention of Saul (who will be later known as Paul, the Greek name for Saul), and it indicates that the death of Stephen must have made an impact on Paul and prepared him for his own encounter with the risen Jesus. How could the witnessing of Stephen's death prepare Paul's heart for repentance and faith?

- Jesus desires oneness among the Father, himself, and believers so that the love that unites them may make God known to the world. How have you experienced this loving unity revealing God to those who do not know him?

- The unity of the Church in the early centuries was a powerful sign of its divine origin and was a major reason for its rapid growth. Why, then, is working for greater unity among Christians today an essential part of the Church's mission?

ORATIO

ᴧ

Jesus prayed "that they may all be one, as you, Father, are in me and I in you, that they also may be in us, that the world may believe that you sent me" (John 17:21). Voice your prayer within this mystical unity between the Father and the Son:

Lord of Love, help me to take away the obstacles that prevent me from experiencing unity with you and with your disciples. Make my life a sign and an instrument of that unity for which you prayed. May the divine love that you made visible to the world continue to be revealed through the forgiveness, love, and unity of your Church.

Continue to pray in your own words, seeking to imitate Jesus' intimacy with the Father.

CONTEMPLATIO

Through contemplation, disciples are able to see beyond the historical and factual circumstances of their lives to their divine purpose and thereby experience God's guidance and assistance. Quietly seek the vision of Stephen, who was filled with the Holy Spirit and saw the glory of the Father and Jesus.

OPERATIO

Jesus prays for his disciples because he realizes how difficult it is to achieve unity. We experience disunity in our families, businesses, churches, and communities. We also recognize the negative consequences of such disunity. Because we must not become satisfied with disunity or grow accustomed to it, what can you do this week to work toward unity in one of these groups to which you belong?

Pentecost Sunday

LECTIO

Inhale and exhale slowly, becoming aware of your breathing as you recognize each breath as a gift from God. Breathe in, being filled with the presence of God's Spirit. Breathe out, letting go of all that could distract you from this sacred time.

Begin reading when you feel ready to hear God's voice.

ACTS 2:1-11

When the time for Pentecost was fulfilled, they were all in one place together. And suddenly there came from the sky a noise like a strong driving wind, and it filled the entire house in which they were. Then there appeared to them tongues as of fire, which parted and came to rest on each one of them. And they were all filled with the Holy Spirit and began to speak in different tongues, as the Spirit enabled them to proclaim.

Now there were devout Jews from every nation under heaven staying in Jerusalem. At this sound, they gathered in a large crowd, but they were confused because each one heard them speaking in his own language. They were astounded, and in amazement they asked, "Are not all these people who are speaking Galileans? Then how does each of us hear them in his native language? We are Parthians, Medes, and Elamites, inhabitants of Mesopotamia, Judea and Cappadocia, Pontus and Asia, Phrygia and Pamphylia, Egypt and the districts of Libya near Cyrene, as well as travelers from Rome, both Jews and converts to Judaism, Cretans and Arabs, yet we hear them speaking in our own tongues of the mighty acts of God."

⋀

Luke's Gospel and his Acts of the Apostles show that Pentecost is the last of three stages in Jesus' relationship with the Spirit. The first begins with Jesus' conception by Mary through the power of the Holy Spirit. The second begins with Jesus' baptism, when he is anointed with the Spirit and confirmed as the Messiah. The third begins with his death and resurrection, and it is unfolded in his ascension and Pentecost. The saving life of Jesus comes to its completion with Pentecost. The One who was first filled with the Holy Spirit now sends the Spirit and clothes his disciples with power from on high.

Jesus said in Luke's Gospel, "I have come to set the earth on fire" (12:49), a declaration that reads like Jesus' personal mission statement. In addition to his mission of bringing good news to the poor, sight to the blind, and freedom for the oppressed, he has come to bring fire to the world. The image of fire can represent different things in the biblical literature. The prophets associated fire with God's word. As Jeremiah prophesied, "Is not my word like fire?" (23:29). The author of Sirach wrote, "Until like fire a prophet appeared, / his words a flaming furnace" (48:1). Fire is also an image in the Hebrew Scriptures of God refining and purifying his people, as fire separates the impurities from precious metals. Only what is precious is tested by fire to purify it: gold among material things and faith among spiritual realities. The mission of

Jesus is to release people from the dross of evil and sin, to proclaim God's word of repentance and good news, and to purify them with a refiner's fire so that they will shine as God's precious treasure. Jesus expresses his desire that his mission be under way: "How I wish it were already blazing!" (Luke 12:49). But before his mission can be accomplished, Jesus must be "baptized" in suffering (12:50), that is, plunged into his agony and death. Through the baptism of his passion, Jesus will baptize God's people "with the holy Spirit and fire" (3:16).

The fire of God's Spirit first accomplishes its purifying effects; then it warms us with God's affection and sets us aflame with fervor. The radical change experienced by the fearful disciples when they receive the Holy Spirit demonstrates the transforming effects of the Spirit's fire. The remedy for lukewarm, apathetic Christianity is the gift of the Holy Spirit. The flame of the Spirit enlightens our mind with wisdom and enkindles our hearts with zeal.

JOHN 14:15-16, 23B-26*

Jesus said to his disciples: "If you love me, you will keep my commandments. And I will ask the Father, and he will give you another Advocate to be with you always.

"Whoever loves me will keep my word, and my Father will love him, and we will come to him and make our dwelling with him. Those who do not love me do not keep my words; yet the word you hear is not mine but that of the Father who sent me.

---

*John 20:19-23, used for Pentecost Sunday, Year A, is also an option for Year C.

"I have told you this while I am with you. The Advocate, the Holy Spirit whom the Father will send in my name, will teach you everything and remind you of all that I told you."

∧

As the earthly life of Jesus draws to a close and he prepares his disciples for his departure, Jesus assures the disciples that he will not leave them alone. Even though he is departing from them, he promises that he and the Father will come to them and dwell with them through the Holy Spirit. In this new era, the living Jesus will be closer to his disciples than ever before.

In Jesus' final discourse, he calls the Holy Spirit the "Paraclete," a Greek word that is translated in various ways: "Advocate," "Helper," "Counselor," "Comforter," and "Consoler." The word literally means "one called to the side of another." The Spirit will do for the disciples what Jesus himself did for them when he was living in their midst—especially teaching and encouraging them. The Advocate will illuminate the revelation from God that Jesus brought to them and apply it to the ever-changing needs of the community.

The presence of this consoling Comforter will be as near as one's own breath. As Jesus speaks to those whom he loves about their oneness with him and with the Father who sent him, he speaks of mutual indwelling. Jesus and the Father will dwell with the believers, making their home with them. This indwelling is through the Holy Spirit who will be with the disciples in the Church forever.

MEDITATIO

Allow God's Spirit, who inspired these holy texts, to work deeply within you as you meditate upon them. Try to assimilate these Scriptures in all their depth so that you can respond to them with your life.

- What is the relationship of the feasts of the Annunciation, the Baptism of Jesus, and Pentecost to one another? Why is Pentecost the conclusion of the liturgical season of Easter?

- What do you think Jesus means by his mission statement, "I have come to set the earth on fire" (Luke 12:49)? What is the role of his Church in making it blaze and spread?

- In the Jewish calendar, Pentecost (or Weeks) celebrates the giving of the Torah to Moses fifty days after Passover, which celebrates the exodus of the Israelites from Egypt. In the Christian calendar, Pentecost occurs fifty days after Easter and marks the end and final goal of the Easter season. What are some of the parallels between the Jewish and Christian feasts? In what ways is Pentecost a completion of Easter?

- What are some of the various meanings of "Paraclete"? How have you experienced the Holy Spirit in these ways?

- Jesus says to us, "The Holy Spirit whom the Father will send in my name, will teach you everything and remind you of all that I told you" (John 14:26). In what ways have you experienced the Holy Spirit teaching you and reminding you as you study the Scriptures?

ORATIO

It is God's grace within us that gives us a desire to pray. Respond to the word of God that you have heard by lifting up your voice to him and expressing what is in your heart:

Come, Holy Spirit, fill the hearts of your faithful, and enkindle in them the fire of your love. Give me a spirit of courage and fervor, and sanctify my heart for the glory of God's kingdom. Guide me as I reflect on the Scriptures you have inspired, and continue your revealing work within me.

Continue to pray in your own words, seeking to imitate Jesus' complete trust in the Father.

CONTEMPLATIO

Through the Holy Spirit, the Father and the Son will make their home within us, dwelling intimately within us like our own breath. In silent stillness, listen to the sound of your own breath and experience the indwelling of God. Trust that God's Spirit is filling you with eternal life and abundant spiritual gifts.

OPERATIO

Although Easter could leave us meditating in wonder at the entrance of the empty tomb, Pentecost awakens us to the startling communal dimension of our faith. We know that the risen Lord continues to work with his immense, sinful, and gifted Church to heal a wounded world. Celebrate Pentecost with new fervor, and then determine how you will continue to practice lectio divina through your life in the Spirit.

Calendar of
Sunday Lectionary Cycles

The lectionary cycle for the Sunday liturgical readings begins each year on the First Sunday of Advent and ends each year on the last Sunday of Ordinary Time, which is the Solemnity of Christ the King. Here are the cycles that will be used by the Church through 2023.

Advent 2012 to Christ the King 2013: Year C

Advent 2013 to Christ the King 2014: Year A

Advent 2014 to Christ the King 2015: Year B

Advent 2015 to Christ the King 2016: Year C

Advent 2016 to Christ the King 2017: Year A

Advent 2017 to Christ the King 2018: Year B

Advent 2018 to Christ the King 2019: Year C

Advent 2019 to Christ the King 2020: Year A

Advent 2020 to Christ the King 2021: Year B

Advent 2021 to Christ the King 2022: Year C

Advent 2022 to Christ the King 2023: Year A

Conversing with God Lectio Divina Series

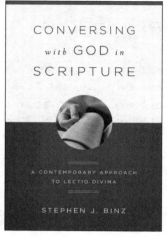

Conversing with God in Scripture:
A Contemporary Approach to *Lectio Divina*

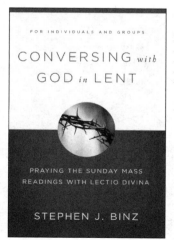

Conversing with God in Lent:
Praying the Sunday Mass Readings with *Lectio Divina*

From The Word Among Us Press

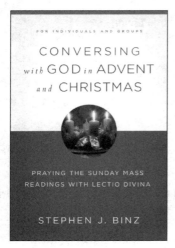

Conversing with God in Advent and Christmas: Praying the Sunday Mass Readings with *Lectio Divina*

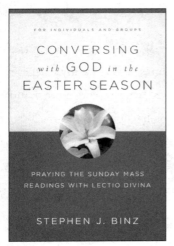

Conversing with God in the Easter Season: Praying the Sunday Mass Readings with *Lectio Divina*

the WORD among us ®
The *Spirit* of Catholic Living

This book was published by The Word Among Us. For more than thirty years, The Word Among Us has been answering the call of the Second Vatican Council to help Catholic laypeople encounter Christ in the Scriptures—a call reiterated recently by Pope Benedict XVI and a Synod of Bishops.

The name of our company comes from the prologue to the Gospel of John and reflects the vision and purpose of all of our publications: to be an instrument of the Spirit, whose desire is to manifest Jesus' presence in and to the children of God. In this way, we hope to contribute to the Church's ongoing mission of proclaiming the gospel to the world and growing ever more deeply in our love for the Lord.

Our monthly devotional magazine, *The Word Among Us*, features meditations on the daily and Sunday Mass readings, and currently reaches more than one million Catholics in North America each year and another 500,000 Catholics in 100 countries. Our press division has published nearly 200 books and Bible studies over the past 12 years.

To learn more about who we are and what we publish, log on to our Web site at **www.wau.org**. There you will find a variety of Catholic resources that will help you grow in your faith.

Embrace His Word, Listen to God . . .